Turtle on a Post

Turtle on a Post

by Carl Parker

as told to Jim Sanderson

LITERARY PRESS
LAMAR UNIVERSITY

ISBN: 978-1-962148-06-1
Library of Congress Control Number: 2024937065

Cover Design: Peyton Garrett
Editors: Dr. Charles Gongre, Emma Hintzen, Christine Osborne, John
Rutherford

Lamar University Literary Press
Beaumont, TX

This title derives from an old joke. A rancher or farmer goes out to his fence and sees his neighbor. They see a turtle on a fence post. The rancher tells his neighbor: "He didn't get up there by himself. And he ain't going to get anything done while he's up there. And you just want to help him down." The joke is in a slightly different form in Wikipedia. There's no telling how old the joke is. Mark Twain, Alex Haley, George W. Bush, Bill Clinton, Barrack Obama, and Donald Trump have all used or are credited with telling the joke.

Recent Prose by Lamar University Literary Press

Robert Bonazzi, *Awakened by Surprise*
Randolph Feezell, *Beyond the Fields*
David Bowles, *Border Lore: Folktales and Legends of South Texas*
Kevin K. Casey, *Four-Peace*
Terry Dalrymple, *Love Stories (Sort of)*
Gerald Duff, *Legends of Lost Man Marsh*
Randolph Feezell, *Beyond the Fields*
Britt Haraway, *Early Men*
Michael Howarth, *Fair Weather Ninjas*
Gretchen Johnson, *The Joy of Deception*
Tom Mack & Andrew Geyer, *A Shared Voice*
Moumin Quazi, *Migratory Words*
Harold Raley, *Lost River Anthology*
Harold Raley, *Louisiana Rogue*
Jim Sanderson, *Trashy Behavior*
Jan Seale, *A Lifetime of Words*
Jan Seale, *Appearances*
Jan Seale, *Ordinary Charms*
C.W Smith, *The Museum of Marriage*
Melvin Sterne, *The Number You Have Reached*
Melvin Sterne, *Redemption*
Melvin Sterne, *The Shoeshine Boy*
John Wegner, *Love Is Not a Dirty Word*

CONTENTS

9   Preface

13   Part I: Before Politics

43   Part II: The House

87   Part III: The Senate

127   Part IV: The Indictment

143   Part V: Practicing Law

169   An Extraordinary Life for an Ordinary Man

Special Thanks

The author would like to thank the following people for their contributions to this book:

Dr. Charles Gongre for copyediting
Peyton Garrett for cover design
Emma Hintzen for proofreading

Preface

I never claimed to be a writer. But sometimes people would introduce me or refer to me as a "writer." The fact that I had published books and stories sometimes slipped out into the place where I worked or the public in general. Sometimes, I was referred to as a "famous arthur." Those labels opened me up to a lot of proposals. The most popular one is that some solicitor has this really great idea for a story or a book or a novel. He will tell me the idea, and I, in turn, will write it up. We would then share the profits. So when my office got a call from Carl Parker, I thought that I was going to get another offer like the one that I describe.

Then I realized, when I returned the call, that this Carl Parker was the Carl Parker whose name was on buildings all around me. So I thought that I better reconsider. Carl did indeed have a writing project in mind, but he wasn't sure what he had. And being an employee of Lamar University and a citizen of Jefferson County, I knew who Carl Parker was. A lot of people didn't know Carl or had forgotten him or had given into labelling him as this or that. So I asked to see what he had.

What he had was bits and pieces of anecdotes. I showed them around. There was not much interest. But I got interested. These bits and pieces were not really political commentary but funny anecdotes. I also started to see a chronological organization based on Carl Parker's growing up and subsequent careers. Then, I realized that I was now on the opposite side of that proposal from the guy with an idea. I was the one with the idea, and Carl had already done most of the writing.

According to my university, if Carl was to use me then the university had to get something from my efforts, as if I were a computer or building or livestock. I'm sure that the expectation of profit was involved. No profit or a lot seemed to be the best options. So my university, Carl, and I came up with a solution. This would be an "as told to" book. But the "as told to part" really wasn't told to me. Carl wanted to leave some notes to his children and grandchildren about one of his political/legal career and problems. He wanted to give his opinion or experience so that his children and grandchildren wouldn't be relying solely on labels.

So Carl had dictated to several people. As he dictated, Carl got more ideas. By the time I came on board, Carl's wife, Beverly, who probably worked harder than all of us, made Carl's dictation into a written electronic document. In turn, rather than being told,

I read the words that Beverly made. Carl's idea was that he just needed some help to get his notes in order and then he was going to leave them to the Museum of the Gulf Coast in Port Arthur for some future scholar. My idea was that we ought to try to make a publishable book. So we would hope for publication, but short of that, Carl would have some important notes. Sure enough, for the first time in my life, I wasn't going to be paid for the words but for the idea. The job was going to work out as all those solicitors suggested.

I began to make a book by reading rather than by writing. My job was cut and paste and edit and organize. I even found the idea for the story in the words that I had. As I began reading, what occurred to me was that this was not at all a political document. Sure, Carl's political beliefs, maneuvers, disappointments, and successes are in the book. But the politics aren't as important as the human stories. There were characters here. I urged Carl to flesh them out. I asked for anecdotes or stories. I asked him to keep telling and keep Beverly word processing. In a sense, I gave a state leader with over fifty years of public service at a variety of levels homework.

But I was careful not to grade too severely. Carl has a sardonic, Texas-style wit. And that wit affects the way he talks. So although readers won't hear Carl, I hope that they can imagine hearing him. I wanted to preserve as much of Carl's way of talking as possible. So rather than read and edit; I tried to hear and edit.

As I read, I saw similarities between Carl and me. Whatever aspirations we might have had, neither Carl nor I could escape Texas. I don't mean just physically. Texas was so much a part of us that we could not even have it surgically removed. His Texas is different from mine. But that Texas experience is like a body part.

We both came from worlds where work meant sweat, hands- on, tools, grime, dirt. We came from places that were blue-collar, union, Texas liberal, worlds that had little in common with a national or more common meaning of "liberal," in a political, philosophical, intellectual, social, or humanistic sense. I wanted to get away from where I had come from. I wanted to get away from work. I wanted to get away from a mind-set. I imagine Carl did too. Neither one of us really did though I live with slightly rarified academic air around me. So we are both physically back where we began, but it is more than that. That Texas liberalism is in us even if we tried to get rid of it. At least for me, I don't like the Texas that is in me, but nor do I want to give it up. I can't vouch for Carl, but I think that he would agree.

Also, for both of us and Beverly, and maybe for my wife, Liz, who saw some of this process, this is a nostalgia piece, especially given what I said above. Carl's intent was to leave a reckoning. That is a present tense reckoning. As Carl composed and Beverly wrote and I organized, we were either creating or recreating a past. We were both here and now, thinking about here and now and back then too. We want to account for change, to stop it for just awhile. To be there but to be free from it.

On a simpler level, Carl has made a social history of a big slice of Texas political life. And mixed in with that recounting are particular places from particular times: The Texas capitol building, Austin, Houston, Port Arthur, union halls, the intercostal canal, deep East Texas.

Finally, and most important, despite the work involved or because of the work involved, I think that both Carl and I want this book to be fun. Readers, I hope, will have a good time reading and will laugh while they are reading.

So I hope that I provided a little bit of an idea about how this book/anecdotes/memoir came about and what it is about.

Part I: Before Politics

Opening note: To my children and grandchildren:

I have written this little essay to give you an idea from whence we all came. You should know how much I love you and am so proud of all my children and grandchildren. I am pleased that all my children have at least two college degrees, and it appears that my grandchildren are on the same route to a fine education. As you may know, in my professional and elected activities, I've always tried to advance and help education.

We are all fortunate to have inherited wonderful genes from our ancestors. Whether we inherited them, learned them, or found them, we got their principles to live by too.

Mom Parker was like a pioneer woman. She was widowed in her late twenties or early thirties, left with six children and a small farm. She survived by farming, using her children, picking cotton for other farmers along with her three boys and three girls. She drove a school wagon every morning to haul children to school. She was a dedicated Church of Christ member, had a sense of humor, was devoted to her children, and ultimately to her grandchildren. She endowed her children with a will to be independent, to work hard, to be honest, and to appreciate others less fortunate than them.

The Christian family was somewhat more genteel, more like plantation owners of earlier times. Mama Christian had had nurse's training but did not finish nursing school. She was a great caretaker for her mother-in-law Great Grandma Christian who lived into her late 90s. Mama Christian was dedicated to her family and to the Baptist church where she played the piano. Mama Christian was a Norris; her father owned a general store in north Louisiana and served 12 years in the Louisiana legislature.

Granddaddy Christian was a politician and close ally of Huey P. Long. Granddaddy was a justice of the police before he was a police juryman (the same as a county commissioner in Texas) and an elder in the Presbyterian church. He was helpful to almost everyone. Granddaddy had a talent for being able to assess timber. He could walk through a grove of trees and within just a few feet estimate the amount of timber that could be taken. Until he was not able to walk, he was employed regularly by people who wanted to know the value of their timber. He was a loving grandfather, proud of all his grandchildren as well as his children. Never forget any of our ancestors.

I am so proud of my children that I get in trouble with my wife who chastises me regularly about my propensity to brag about my children and grandchildren. I feel comfortable that in the future you will all continue to make our name something that everyone is proud of. I would hope that someday you can share my pride with your grandchildren, and I hope that you will share this writing with them.

A Different Time, A Different World

Having lived well now eighty-six years, I have the opportunity to step back in time to see what seems to me now as a complete other world. Sometimes, it seems that the only connection between the place and time that I now live in and the place and time that I was raised is me. And not really even me but some vivid images or stories in my memory.

Juanita Parker

Juanita Parker, my mother, is special because she is so typical of women at a certain time and place. Juanita Parker grew up the daughter of Von and Winnie Christian, a typical old-South family. The Christian family were farmers, raising cotton, corn, and all other produce necessary to sustain life in the later 1800s and early 1900s. Von and Winnie Christian had three daughters and one son. Juanita, apparently was adventuresome for her time, enjoying driving her grandfather's Model-T vehicle, playing basketball as a jumper on the Oak Grove girls' basketball team, clad as she described it in black stockings and bloomers.

Juanita graduated at the top of a fairly small class in Oak Grove High School, but could only obtain a job as cook and housekeeper for her grandmother for a girl her age and experience. To assist her father she acted as his secretarial help, pecking out letters and other documents on the typewriter while Von Christian, her father, acted as Justice of the Peace for DeSoto Parish, Louisiana.

In August 1933, Harvie Parker hired a friend to drive him to North Louisiana where he retrieved Juanita Parker with a proposal of marriage. At the time Juanita was visiting relatives but accepted the proposal; the three of them, Harvie, Juanita, and the owner of the car, traveled to Mansfield where Juanita purchased a white dress; Harvie purchased a marriage license and found a retired preacher to perform the ceremony. They then departed Louisiana for Port Arthur, Texas, which was to be their home for the rest of their lives. Their honeymoon night was spent on the couch in the living room of Harvie's sister's one bedroom duplex on Houston Avenue in Port Arthur, Texas.

With her intellect and drive, Juanita could have been anything she wanted to be had she been able to go to college. Instead, she did what women at the time did.

Harvie Parker

Harvie Parker was born on May 19, 1910, in a little community about 5 miles out of Logansport, Louisiana. The community was noted for the name of its school, Oak Grove School. It was not incorporated; and later, after being incorporated, it became known as Stanley, Louisiana. Harvie died of lung cancer January 28, 1981. Harvie was the third of five children born to J. C. Parker and Chloe Parker. His dad died when he was approximately 11 years old, leaving Chloe with 5 children and some farmland. Chloe, with the help of her brothers, Tom and Will, and the children, farmed the land and scratched out a living. For a little cash, she drove a school wagon which would set out before daylight and gather children to take to the Oak Grove School. By age 14, Harvie dropped out of school and started driving a Model-T dump truck hauling gravel to help support the family.

Harvie was a gangly type of fellow, about 6'2", long and lanky. He was not to fill out into the man he became until after he reached about 18 years old. Harvie and all his brothers and sisters ended up being well acquainted with hard work. Not only did they farm their own land, but they hired out to other farmers and relatives to chop, pick cotton and other agricultural duties. Addie Mae, the oldest sibling, eventually wrote a history of the family and described how Chloe and all of her older children would work the fields while Tressie, the second youngest, would babysit Feeler, who was still a babe-in-arms, under the shade of a tree near the field.

By the time Harvie was in his late teens, he and relatives had hoboed by hopping freight trains and traveling throughout West and South Texas as well as part of Louisiana picking cotton and looking for pulpwood and making crossties. He eventually, at age 17, joined his brother, Ferral, who had moved to Port Arthur, Texas, looking for work in the refineries. After a short stint with Texaco, Harvie got on with the Gulf Oil Company where he stayed employed for forty years, taking an early retirement at age 57.

When Harvie finally landed a steady job at Gulf, he was earning all of 35 cents an hour and for the most part walking to work. Mother said that when they married, he had approximately $8.00 in the bank. She promptly spent $2.00 on an alarm clock so she could get him to work on time.

Harvie's sense of hard work and dedication to his job was quite apparent. The only time I recall him missing a day off from work from the Gulf Refinery was when he broke his leg on the job. He spent 40 years doing shift work, alternating the day shift from 7 a.m. to 3 p.m. with the 3 p.m. to 11 p.m. and then 11 p.m. to 7 a.m. in alternate weeks. I hardly ever remember him sleeping more than 2-3 hours when coming off a graveyard or 11 p.m -7 a.m. shift.

Harvie Parker was an industrious fellow, always having some sideline to earn more money for the family. The first I recall was during WWII when transportation was at a minimum. The war effort had taken all the new vehicles. You could not buy a new car, and old cars which would run were at a premium. In his on-going belief he could do anything, Harvie began to amass some old junker cars, the first of which was a 1936 model Plymouth limousine. He would take the cars, put them in sound running order, and sell them for a large profit. When it became apparent he could make more money if the car's body presented a nice appearance, Harvie enrolled as a sedaline welder. He learned to patch the old car's rusted-out parts, fill them in with lead, grind them down and spray-paint a new coat of paint on the cars. Although Harvie did well at the re-conditioned car business, he was soon to be off to another venture after the war ended. He and his brother-in-law, Dalton Tolley, bought twin, flat-bed, 2-ton trucks and started seeking ways to earn money with the trucks.

Their first venture was to drive down to Rio Grande Valley and return with two trucks loaded with watermelons. These were marketed in Dalton Tolley's front yard which was on a busy street then known as 16th Street or Gulfway Drive. Tolley, as we called him, was married to Dovey, another of Harvie's sisters.

Unionization was pretty much a religion with Harvie. He worked long hours, even on his vacation, trying to adjust grievances of his fellow union members. He was recognized as a national union leader by President Harry Truman who appointed him to be one of the United States' representatives at the World Labor Congress in Venezuela. Harvie was always neck deep in politics, chairing the political action committee for his union on many occasions, eventually seeking a seat on the city council of Port Arthur. His first venture in politics was a losing one, having lost the election to city council by two votes. Even after several re-counts, the two-vote margin held for his opponent. Eventually, he was elected to city council and then elevated to serve as mayor of the city of Port Arthur.

Harvie's stint as mayor included having to evacuate the city for a hurricane wherein he stayed throughout the crisis, which led him to cooperate and urge Congressman Jack Brooks, his political ally, to construct the seawall protection around the city of Port Arthur, which has saved our city on numerous occasions since.

Harvie Parker was full of pithy sayings. His humor bordered on barnyard, sometimes vulgar, but his quotes were usually cogent. What Harvie Parker had to say about a person he held in lowest esteem with no redeeming social value was, "He was the kind of person you couldn't trust in an outhouse with a muzzle on." He was also very dedicated about his unionism and believed anyone who would cross a picket line was despicable and not worthy of any respect whatsoever. During a very long strike at the Texaco Refinery, a neighbor of ours named McMahon chose to cross the picket line— or as my dad said, "scab" the union. On his way to work on his bicycle one morning, he was interrupted by 5 guys who delivered a pretty sound beating to him. I confronted my dad about it saying, "Although I'm on the union's side, it doesn't seem a fair fight for 5 against 1."

Harvie pointed out to me, "Son, you're confused. They didn't want to fight with him; they wanted to give him a whipping." Which they in fact did. Some of his other country sayings involved an observation of any building or object that seemed to be off center, he would say, "It was leaning toward Joneses." Someone very rich, he'd say, "He was richer than Ben Gump." Leary of a braggart, he told me "A guy who tells how rich or how religious he is, usually ain't!'"

Juanita and Harvie Parker told me that I was born in Port Arthur at 4:50 a.m., August 6, 1934. I was delivered by Dr. White in a small frame house in the 100 block of 15th Street. Apparently, at the time, going to the hospital wasn't an option for my 19-year-old mother. I heard repeated stories, particularly from my father, about how he was working 10-hour shifts at the refinery, changing and washing my dirty diapers, while at the same time nursing my mother who had contracted diphtheria. He always embellished the story by saying he did it all with a huge carbuncle on his elbow which kept him in excruciating pain throughout the experience.

17

My first recollection, independent of yarns told by my parents and other relatives about my early childhood, was living on Main Avenue in what is now Groves. My father, having been raised as a country boy, had strong desires to try to live as close to his former lifestyle as possible. So he bought two large lots in a subdivision off Main Avenue called Garden Farms. With the help and advice of some carpenter friends and occasionally a hired carpenter, my dad built the small frame house consisting of two bedrooms, a living room, and kitchen. It also had a free-standing garage. Our bathroom facilities were located about 50 feet directly behind the house in what also served as the chicken yard and the pen for the cow.

My memories of those days were snapshots and mostly pleasant. I suppose this goes to show the old adage that you tend to remember the good and erase the bad from your memory. Every day brought some new adventure. My dad would show me some of the things which amused him as a child. I recall us building a boiler out of a syrup bucket, creating a fireplace underneath it, filling it half full of water with small holes in the top of it, and heating it until it would whistle and blow steam. On one hunting trip, he captured a baby raccoon and brought it home where we kept it in a chicken coop for some time, mostly for our amusement. I was filled with awe by the way my dad could milk a cow (two-hands at a time). I would often hold the bucket for him. I fed the chickens and watched my parents plant a huge garden. We dug up an elm tree near my grandparents' home in Northern Louisiana and planted it in our yard. I nurtured that tree by carrying buckets of water in the summertime every day to water it. The tree still stands today as a fairly large tree.

We had trouble with well water. It did not taste good and was so hard that it was almost impossible to make lather with soap. My mother did the best she could with it, washing clothes by hand on a scrub board for a long time before we finally got the first wringer washing machine. Our drinking water was caught off the roof by gutters running into a large tin cistern which sat about ten feet off the ground on a platform. Because of the mosquitoes and wiggle tails, mother would always have to boil our water used for cooking or drinking. We were so far out in the country at that time that I had recollections of following my dad with his English Pointer bird dog, hunting birds on the west side of Main Avenue. Smith's dairy was just up the road, and we would make the annual trip to have our milk cow dipped when Mister Smith ran his cows through his dipping vat. We eventually got city water and indoor plumbing.

A ditch in front of our house provided me adventure and play. I caught crawfish with bacon on a string, imagined myself in the trenches of World War I and to the horror of my mother, attempted to float the length of the ditch in a huge rainstorm in one of her wash tubs. Then I watched the equipment go down Main Avenue to dig a city ditch and cover my drainage ditch.

My parents bought me a bicycle from Sears (an Elgin). Teaching me to ride it and watching my mother trying to master it herself amused me and my father. My dad bought me a horse. And imagining myself a cowboy, I explored most of that part of the community and watched as my dad tried to make my little saddle horse plow his garden. When the horse wouldn't pull, my dad popped him on the butt with the reigns. My horse took off—plow, traces, and all and ran through the chicken yard fence. My dad went back to a push garden hoe plow after that.

Christmastime, we had small, home-decorated Christmas trees. Cold weather wasn't much fun; I would bathe in a No. 2 washtub placed beside our wood stove for heat. It would be terribly hot on one side and completely cold on the other. Trips to the outdoor privy by the light of my dad's flashlight were certainly frightening for a small child. I wondered what spiders or other creepy-crawlies were sharing the facilities with me. My mother was my main playmate, teaching me to play ball, knit, crochet and even cook a little. She read to me a lot—book after book, particularly at times when I was down with childhood diseases like the measles. I still remember her recitations of *Robinson Crusoe, Swiss Family Robinson,* and *Huckleberry Finn.* Of course, Bible verses were always a big part of my mother's reading as well. She expected me to memorize word-for-word each one. I wasn't sure at the time whether it was so much that she was contributing to my religious training or just wanted to show me off to all the other relatives about how well I could recite from memory.

I entered Franklin School in the third grade. Franklin was a real challenge.

Franklin School

Having started school in Port Neches School District at Groves Elementary, I was somewhat traumatized when I was transferred to Franklin Elementary in Port Arthur.

The hobby at Franklin among the boys seemed to be fisticuffs. The first day I entered Franklin, while getting a sip of water from a fountain, I was suddenly whacked on the back of my head, forcing my mouth into the spigot. As I rose, a fellow was standing there who said, "My name is Tommy Becker and I can whip you."

19

I quickly learned that almost all the boys had to be tested so that the pecking order of who could whip who could be established. I had a daily battle with others in my class. Franklin was so combative I used to joke that there was a sign on the playground saying, "If you can't fight, help tote off the dead."

I relayed this story to my wife, Beverly, who raised her eyebrows in doubt. Several years later, as we were campaigning for the Senate, Beverly and I were making the rounds in Dayton, Texas. We entered a barber shop where I proceeded to hand out my push cards. One of the barbers looked at me, looked at the card and asked, "Are those boys in Port Arthur the sissies they used to be?"

I quickly replied, "Mister, you don't understand, where I went to grade school there was a sign on the playground saying, 'If you can't fight help tote off the dead.'"

He grinned and looked at me and replied, "You went to Franklin School." Beverly seemed to be satisfied with this verification of my yarn about my grade school days.

Country Boy in the City

As a small child, I would visit my grandparents, Momma and Granddaddy Christian and Mom Parker, in Oak Grove, Louisiana. Mom Parker lived alone in a house unpainted with a dog run in the middle. A dog run was an open space with bedrooms and other rooms on either side to allow the free flow of air in the summertime. In Texas a dog run is not a Texas style but a southern style. Air conditioning was not known in Oak Grove, Louisiana when I was a small child.

My memories of Mom Parker are very fond in that she was a widow lady, living alone except for her youngest son Thealer, known to us as Uncle Red. Uncle Red still farmed fields adjacent to Mom Parker's house growing corn and cotton, and he had a fairly good-sized garden growing vegetables to live on. Mom Parker also had a small herd of milk cows which she would call up in the evening by hollering in a loud voice, "Sous Cow." Cows would come running for their evening meal and to be milked as they had been in the morning. Mom Parker had no running water in the house, no gas, and no electricity. A fireplace and wood burning iron stove furnished heat. With no chicken pen, chickens ran throughout the yard but would return to the chicken house in the evening for the purpose of laying eggs which Mom Parker would gather daily. There was no indoor plumbing, and while there, I was forced to use a wooden outdoor privy equipped with past issues of Sears catalogs to use for toilet paper. Mom Parker's house was built on the very same ground now occupied by our round house in Louisiana.

One of my chores when visiting Mom Parker was to go outside and clip small twigs from sweet gum trees to serve her as a brush. She would chew the end until it looked feathery, then wet it in her mouth and dip it in a box of Garrett Snuff. Mom Parker always kept an ample supply of Garrett, and the gum tree bush full of it stuck inside her jaw. Mom Parker had the Parker sense of humor and her own ways of discipling her rowdy grandchildren, particularly the boys. I recall that, if I was causing too great a disturbance, along with my male cousins, Mom Parker would take us in the house, put the cuffs of our pants under the leg of her chair, and hold us captive until we promised to behave. If we were being too insolent, she would threaten to lock us in the closet with some creature known only to us, as described by Mom Parker, as Raw Head and Bloody Bones. It was enough to scare the daylights out of us and cause us to behave for a while.

The community where Mom Parker and the Christians lived was known as Oak Grove. It was an unincorporated section of land called Oak Grove because of the name of the school. Grandma and Granddaddy went to Oak Grove School. Grandma was valedictorian of her class. Granddaddy dropped out in the ninth grade to work to help support his family. Oak Grove was located on about a ten or fifteen acre strand between Logansport, which was on the boundary of Texas and Mansfield, further east on the road. While I was a child, the road was made up of hard gravel, and though it would be grated occasionally to smooth it out, it was covered with big rock gravel which after a short time of traffic would gather between the ruts in piles of rock about a foot tall in some instances. Side roads were mostly dirt and paved roads in that area were almost non-existent.

Momma and Granddaddy lived about nine miles east of Mom Parker on the same road. Visiting the Christian grandparents was truly an experience akin to olden times.

Like Mom Parker, the Christian household had no electricity. They depended on kerosene lamps, and I recall a step forward when the Aladdin lamp was invented and Momma and Granddaddy purchased one. The early kerosene lamps were composed of a cloth wick that descended into the bowl of kerosene and could be rolled up by a roller giving greater or lesser flame and light. The Aladdin lamp was an improvement in that instead of a cloth wick, a small net-type piece was above the supply of kerosene, and the kerosene would go up into the net and when lit, it would produce a much brighter glow than a simple flame from a single wick.

Heat in Momma and Granddaddy's house was also furnished by a huge fireplace in the living room and a cast iron stove in the kitchen. Momma would faithfully cook biscuits almost every morning in the cast iron stove and serve them up along with oatmeal, baked apples, scrambled eggs, bacon, and ham.

Momma and Granddaddy always supplied butter, and while I was visiting, I always enjoyed operating the churn. The churn was a large crock with a lid that had a hole in the middle. A plunger with handles sticking through the hole in the middle allowed me to work it up and down, sloshing the raw milk until the butter appeared at the top and could be skimmed off and placed in pats and later served with meals. One of Momma Christian's delicacies, which she would share on Sundays and all special occasions, was her homemade yeast rolls.

The Christian house was surrounded by corn and cotton fields with a large field of sugar cane. Granddaddy farmed the old-fashioned way with horse or mule drawn plows, rakes and other farming tools. There was a large corral in the rear of the house with a barn and a large feed trough. The barn had a shed with a long pole hanging from wires running from one side of the barn to the other. In the evening, when the horses and mules were unhitched from their plowing duties, Granddaddy hung the horse collars, reins, bridles and paraphernalia on the pole. Corn and meal were spread in the trough to feed the horses and mules. Amusingly, chickens, who ran freely all around the place, would always show up at feeding time to avail themselves of the leftover feed in the cracks and on the ground around the feed trough. The barn crib was usually filled with un-shucked corn and sometimes a good supply of peanut vines. The adults would remind me that eating raw peanuts would give me a bellyache. I ate a lot of those peanuts. I never got a bellyache. My folks endowed me with a strong stomach.

In addition to the barn structure in the rear of the Christian household was a smokehouse and a chicken house. There was a large black washpot immediately in the rear of the house which once a week would be heated with a wooden fire, brought to boil, and filled with the week's laundry. Most of the white items would be boiled in the washpot and then placed in a tin wash tub and sometimes, stains and dirt were scrubbed from the clothing by rubbing them on a wash board comprised of wood and corrugated metal. The smokehouse was the storehouse for smoked meats. Hams and sausages hung from strings in the ceiling, and there was a large box full of rock salt in which slabs of bacon were buried. During hog-killing or cow-butchering time, a small fire was kept burning in the smokehouse to provide the smoke to cure the meat. Adjacent to the home and between it and the cotton fields was a large garden. It contained beans, corn, beets, tomatoes, and every other kind of vegetable you could think of.

I was privileged on occasion to watch the process of providing meat for not only the family but the Black families who lived on the place. The hog would be shot or hit in the head with a large hammer in the hog pen, a pit was dug, and a large fire was built in the pit.

A 55-gallon drum was filled with water and placed pretty much on its side over the fire pit. As the water was brought to a boil, the slain hog would be doused inside the boiling water to allow the removal of the hair from the pig skin. When the hog was skinned, the skin was fried and the result was called cracklings. Every part of the hog except the teeth and toenails, to my recollection, was used. The hog was butchered into roasts, bacon, hams, and other parts. The guts were removed then cleaned out and washed by the women indoors while the men were butchering the hog outdoors. The guts were used as tubes. Ground meat and spices were placed in them to form links of sausage. Later they were hung in the smokehouse to be cured.

Usually about the same time, canning was underway by the women in the family. Vegetables would be cooked and placed in either jars or cans and thereafter placed in a large pressure cooker to further cook and seal the contents of the jars and cans. My favorite among the canning operation was Momma Christian's dewberries and blackberries. Milk was placed in large jars and jugs and lowered to the bottom of a water cistern which supplied water for the family. The cistern was a large, tin tank which caught water off the roof directed into the tank by a gutter system.

Although slavery had long since ended, there was still a form of subjugation of Black people in the Oak Grove area. On his farm, Granddaddy Christian had two or three houses where Black families dwelt. One house was occupied by Leona. Leona had been with the family since she was a child, her parents having worked for my great grandfather Christian on his farm. Leona had three boys and a girl. The boys were old enough that they were the field hands for Granddaddy. Leona's house was an unpainted shack about 100 yards behind their house.

When I visited, I would generally spend almost as much time at Leona's house being entertained by her tales as I did at Momma and Granddaddy's house. Leona kept the house, did a lot of the cooking, cleaned, gathered eggs, and milked the cows. On one occasion, Leona noticed a big seed wart on my thumb. I had that wart as long as I could remember. I thought it was a natural part of my body. Leona told me that she could do away with that seed wart without pain to me. Even though doubtful, I followed her instructions. I gathered her a straw from a straw broom. She sat down and dipped the straw into her mouth where she kept her lower lip full of Garrett Snuff. She would then touch the end of the straw on each seed of the wart on my thumb. Believe it or not, within about a month I had almost forgotten about the incident, but the seed wart was gone.

After Leona got rid of my wart, I spent hours at Leona's house, sometimes late in the evening when her boys would return from the field. Billy, the oldest of the bunch, was a great guitarist, and we would sit on Leona's porch and be entertained by Billy's blues songs. Down the road, a block or two, lived the other family. The head of that family was a Black man known only as Hoonay; it was the only name I ever knew him by. He had no children but was sort of the head field hand, directing the other Black men living on the place in their daily chores.

Granddaddy Christian was an elected official for DeSoto Parrish. He was police juryman, which in Louisiana is the same as a county commissioner. The Commission would meet weekly in Mansfield and oft times Granddaddy would take me to Mansfield with him and invariably would let me attend one of the movie houses in Mansfield while he attended the juryman's meeting. Almost without fail though, being the only grandchild for a few years, I always returned from Mansfield with some gift that Granddaddy would buy me. I recall a croquet set, a Red Ryder BB gun, and numerous other nice gifts.

Granddaddy Christian was an elder in the Presbyterian Church while Momma Christian was a devout Baptist who played the piano at the Baptist church. I would often alternate attending church with Granddaddy one Sunday and Momma Christian the next. I especially enjoyed attending with Granddaddy Christian in that his church had only one room; therefore, the children met for Sunday School outside under an oak tree and later would join the congregation for singing. At Granddaddy's church there was only a circuit preacher who showed up once a month. Generally, he would preach at the Presbyterian church and then join us at Granddaddy

Christian's house for lunch. Momma Christian's church was larger, had adequate rooms for Sunday School classes which I attended when going with her.

I, of course, lived in the city, so I belonged to this world but was not really a part of it. In my memory, it seems vivid but not real. It is such a different time and world compared to our world that it just seems like it was always in my memory, just implanted so to speak, and not ever real.

A Raccoon Hunt

Among my kinfolks, hunting and fishing was a part of developing your manhood. My uncles and cousins also honored self-defense (boxing) and respect for God, women, and our elders. The hunting and fishing part wasn't only for sport, particularly among my uncles as they were growing up. Hunting supplied a significant portion of their food.

Fishing included lots of bank-fishing in ponds, creeks, and rivers. Trotline fishing would usually include groups and campouts on the Sabine River. The results were our outdoor fish fries of perch and catfish.

Though we hunted doves, ducks, and quail, my dad's favorite was squirrel hunting. He was a true woodsman, and I never knew him to get lost no matter what the size of the forest we found ourselves in. Places to hunt squirrels were plentiful. Most of the timberland was not posted for trespassing, and we took full advantage of the timber companies' large areas of wooded acreage. Most of the hunting woods were several miles north of Port Arthur. We would have to rouse about 4:00 a.m. in order to be in the woods by daylight. My dad would threaten to leave me behind if I failed to be up and ready at the appointed time. I recall numerous evenings and nights when I tried my best to stay awake all night to be sure that I was not left behind on these hunting trips. Hunting with my dad was not only one of my favorite things, it was also educational. It taught me a lot about direction, survival, animals, and appreciation of nature. Slithering through the woods stalking game made me feel much like the pioneers of old that I had read about in many books. Some more of my connection to that world was raccoon hunting. My uncles enjoyed raccoon hunting when I was growing up. Addie Mae's husband, Uncle Bill, owned a whole kennel full of hunting dogs. Hunting dogs are generally hounds. Raccoon hunting doesn't necessarily mean you have to catch the raccoon. The fun is learning

25

the voices of the hunting hounds. It is entertaining to discern which hound was in the lead in following the scent of the raccoons. We would occasionally have the dogs tree a wildcat, which we would dispatch on the spot. A treed wildcat is really scary to a city boy. When we would tree raccoons, however, on most occasions, we would try to shake the raccoon out of the tree and enjoy the combat between the raccoon and the dogs. It was usually a short battle in that a trained dog knew exactly how to conquer a raccoon without getting bitten, scratched, or scarred up by a heavy raccoon.

As I was growing up, my best pals at Memorial Church, Grimble and Rudy Robbins, had never participated in a raccoon hunt. They had heard me talking about such a hunt and declared they would certainly be pleased if I would invite them on one. So, I set about to create a hunt for their edification.

I made a deal with my uncle to borrow his hunting dogs. We located a friend who had a little farm up in East Texas, not far out of Mauriceville. He allowed that he would like for us to rid his property of raccoons because they were destroying his corn crop. So, armed with all this information, we set out for the location in East Texas. We arrived about an hour or two after dark and set four of the hounds loose. They immediately scented raccoons in the corn patch where raccoons had laid waste to a large portion of our friend's crop. However, when the dogs smelled the scent, they seemed to go off in four different directions. So, we tried to follow them by splitting up our group and going in different directions, but soon afterward the hounds joined in one line of pursuit. One of the hounds we called Old Dianna. Dianna was the surest of the bunch. When Old Dianna treed, you can be certain there was something in the tree, and you had better stay until you figured out what it was and got it out, or Old Dianna wouldn't leave the tree. Old Dianna had treed, and with her long bark, we could tell it was her.

We set out to find the tree that Old Dianna had spotted for us, and as we approached it and shined our light up in the tree, there were numerous sets of eyes. It appeared that the dogs had treed not only one raccoon but a female raccoon with about four or five little raccoons. They were spread out all over the tree. Grimble and Rudy thought it would be neat to capture one of the babies and see if they could tame it as a pet. So, one of our bunch climbed the tree and managed to shake one of the baby raccoons off. Grimble, who was the older brother of Rudy, but not as tall, grabbed the raccoon by the tail and immediately all four hounds who were there started leaping on him, trying to reach the raccoon. Grimble danced around for a while yelling at Rudy, "Rudy, take this dang thing, you are a lot taller than I am." Rudy did but soon gave up because he was attacked by the hounds as well. We went on to tree another couple of raccoons, but it was a memorable coon hunt, very amusing with antics with Grimble, Rudy, and the hounds, made better because we were city boys experiencing the country.

Junior High School/High School

Junior high school was a different experience for me. Having left the cocoon of friendship and warmth I felt at Franklin School, having at the cost of some pain established myself in the pecking order of things, I ventured into Woodrow Wilson with some trepidation. I was still extra-skinny and not very tall and felt somewhat intimidated by the boys and girls who had come to Woodrow from the "rich" part of town. Almost all of the Hispanic kids at Woodrow and 80% of day laborers and hourly employees' kids came from Franklin with a sprinkle from DeQueen. The rest were children of supervisors, plant managers, and professional folks.

I began to learn in junior high that I did in fact have a flair for humor. As I have learned over the years, humor can be a valuable social tool, but also a dangerous instrument to deal with when not used properly. As a result, my compulsion in junior high was to entertain the teachers with my wit, particularly the young ones right out of college. I am told that I set the record for having had to visit the boys' advisor while attending this institution. While studies generally came fairly easy to me, it was both a blessing and a handicap that I could see no reason to study any harder than I needed to get by. In view of the fact that no one in my entire family had ever thought about going to college, no one had explained to me the importance of studying or even knowing how to study. While both my mother and father tried to help encourage my studies, the emphasis was always on "Did you pass?" not "Did you make an 'A'?"

By now, I had given up walking to school and was allowed to ride my bike. I abhorred the thought of having to carry a school satchel (backpacks were not in vogue at this time), therefore, I had an equal distaste for taking books, notebooks, or other written material home with me from school. It was too big a bother on the bicycle. This slight problem caused me to flunk the only academic course I ever failed in my entire life—seventh grade math. Ms. Watson told me early on, without regard to my passing grades on all of the exams, she would not allow me to pass if I did not begin to turn in my homework. Having made Bs and Cs on the tests, I could not for the life of me see the necessity of turning in useless homework. I didn't, and she did. Having earned a failing grade in math, my father rewarded me by allowing me to attend summer school. For good measure, since I hadn't been a spectacular student of English, my father thought that, since I was going anyway, I may as well take two courses instead of just one—an exercise that taught me several lessons as well as making me much better in math and ultimately in English. Being robbed of the largest part of a barefoot summer was truly cruel and inhumane punishment to me at the time.

Primarily because of my urge to be a class wit and entertain my fellow students as well as the teacher, I was too often referred to the boys' advisor who would generally lecture me about how good I could have been and what I should do. He left little if any impression on me.

Unfortunately, as I progressed to Thomas Jefferson High School, I didn't particularly see the need for any kind of change in my conduct until my first visit to the assistant principal in charge of discipline at the high school. I had been discovered pulling a prank by throwing an apple core through the open second floor window of the high school. When I faced Mr. Duval, the advisor, he informed me that he did not intend to punish me but that I was old enough that the law no longer required that they keep me in school, and since it appeared that I was not really interested in an education, they would just expel me from school and send me home.

It immediately popped in my head what would happen to me when my father learned that I had been expelled from school. This struck my deepest fears. I begged for another chance and promised Mr. Duval that I would never again have the need of his counsel. He relented and allowed me to stay in school, and I was true to my word; I never again was called before the principal or assistant principal for disciplinary reasons.

Primarily due to my mother and father's urging, who had told me early on that I would, in fact, go to college, I signed up for the college bound curriculum in high school. I did have two non-academic courses I was allowed; I signed up for choir and wood shop. Again, I saw no need for constant study, still feeling that as long as I made a "C" that was adequate. I had little, or no, involvement in social activities in high school in that I was generally required to be working immediately after being released from school in the afternoons. First, I assisted my father with his nursery business, and later I worked at my first hourly paid job washing dishes at one of the more popular drive-ins in Port Arthur, Reese's Drive In.

I would go to work at 4:00 after school and work until 10:30 or 11:00 for the princely sum of $0.35 an hour. At the time, there were no mechanical dishwashers, and I was required to wash dishes by hand in a three-stage operation. Clean the dishes, wash them in soapy water first, wash them in germ free solution, and stack them to dry. I found the work miserable, and to this day, I am very reluctant to be hooked into washing dishes anywhere. The job was so delusional and unpleasant that it was the only job that I ever quit in anger.

Fortunately for me, after I resigned my job as dishwasher, I was hired by Mr. Carl Smith at a new soft ice cream store called Zestos. I received a handsome raise; being given $0.50 an hour and all the ice cream I could eat. The job at Zestos I kept for over two years while in high school and allowed me to build up my savings that I intended to use to support my college. The job with Mr. Smith was most pleasant in that he was a very kind gentleman, who taught me a lot about how to deal with people and how to become a good and responsible employee.

I recall on one occasion when I was cleaning up the store, I told Mr. Smith that I had done such a good job that I challenged him to find anything wrong. Well, very shortly he found one spot out of sight that I had not adequately cleaned and pointed it out to me. He then gave me the lesson which I have not ever forgotten; Mr. Smith said it was very foolish to invite anyone to find something wrong with what you have done.

After working for Mr. Smith for some time, I increased my responsibilities so that I was in fact the manager of the facility. The soft ice cream was very popular, and, on some weekends, the gross income was $400-$600 which was spectacular because the most expensive item on our menu was $0.25 for a milkshake or sundae. After graduating from high school, with my dad's help, I was hired by Jefferson County to become the assistant janitor at the Jefferson County sub-Court House in Port Arthur. My duties included cleaning in normal janitorial fashion, keeping the lawn and shrubbery trimmed in and around the courthouse and, also, searching the sub-basement for the source of termites which had eaten the door down in one of the commissioner's offices.

I discovered that upon completing construction of the courthouse in the '20s, the construction crew had not removed the wooden timbers used to form the concrete on the four sets of steps of the courthouse. Unfortunately, the wood became infested with termites which had proceeded up into several of the offices. I was required by my job to tear out the rotten boards, stack them up, and shove them through holes for disposal. It was very dirty work, but we managed to get it done without incident.

One of my other duties was my first experience with the election process. I was transferred temporarily from the sub-courthouse to the storage barn where all the voting machines of the county were kept. The job I was assigned was to take Windex and cleaner and rags and clean the tops of all the voting machines where they had bird droppings deposited on them.

At the end of the summer, I had my savings expanded to $600 when Emilio Rojo, Leopold Villegas, and I loaded into Leo's coupe and headed for Austin to begin our college careers.

Golden Port Arthur

One of the few benefits of aging is memories. One of my long time Port Arthur pals has always shared with me that in his opinion we grew up in the golden years of Port Arthur. I believe it to be true. And many of my childhood and young man memories come back as I drive through various parts of Port Arthur. And those memories, besides being golden, even have a golden tint to them.

In the 40s and 50s, Port Arthur was the source of great jobs, a booming economy, and a quality of life unmatched by most Texas cities or counties. Port Arthur schools in the 40s and 50s had the highest paid teachers in the state. Citizens of our city had the highest per capita income of any city in Texas. Downtown was thriving, and big bands made regular visits to our world-famous ballroom at Pleasure Pier. When I was a boy, my allowance was a dollar, eventually growing to two dollars a week. I could usually earn another couple of bucks mowing my neighbor's yard with their push mowers. A couple of dollars was all I needed to have an enjoyable weekend. I could take the bus downtown and back for fifteen cents. The fare included a transfer back to where I was picked up. Nine cents admitted me to a movie, and hamburgers at Bob's Burger Bar downtown cost a quarter and a coke five cents. Port Arthur enjoyed three movie theaters downtown: the People's, the Strand, and the Pierce. Procter Street was thriving with almost shoulder-to-shoulder people up and down shopping at the various filled and thriving stores. My choice of movies was always the People's that showed a double feature of cowboy shows, a comic, and a serial. Popcorn was a nickel, coke was a nickel, and for two cents you could get an all-day sucker. On Procter Street you could shop at Nacol's Jewelry, Bluestein's Department Store, Pletman's Grocery, Kress's, and Woolworth's, which had a wonderful, large soda fountain. There were two fancy hotels: the Sabine and the Goodhue. The Goodhue's top floor was the location of the Port Arthur Club where all the businessmen gathered for lunches, chamber meetings, poker games, and various other sources of adult entertainment.

In those days there was no organized baseball, so we played "scrub" on some of the numerous vacant lots in the neighborhood, or we traveled to the park for a makeup game against some other neighborhood group. The neighborhood was friendly, and all of us kids had the run of about a four-block area. It was not unusual for us to play in almost anyone's backyard, but we had to watch out for the various clothes lines. Hardly anyone had a clothes dryer, if they even knew they existed. Clothes lines were very prevalent. Our campouts were usually Army surplus "pup" tents that we would pitch and camp out with, build fires in the alley to roast wieners, or toast potatoes thrown in the fire. Texaco Reservoir was our personal swimming hole where many of us learned to swim. It was always a treat when the popsicle man came through the neighborhood with his bell ringing. But an even greater treat was when the Brown Ice Cream Wagon, pulled by a horse, came through. The Brown Ice Cream Wagon was truly a mobile ice cream parlor having various flavors where you could get a double dip ice cream for a nickel or dime.

Port Arthur in those days was truly mid-America. Schools were great, employment was high, and most of our parents, our fathers at least, were employed in one of the two major refineries, or in an occupation directly connected with the refineries. Although there was no television, we had radio programs. Most of us kids would tune in to *Mr. District Attorney, Orphan Annie, Tom Mix,* or *Jack Armstrong-All American Boy.* Family listening always included Fiber McGee and Molly, the news, heavyweight boxing matches, and the Major Bowe's Amateur Hour with Ted Mack.

In the 40s and 50s, Port Arthur probably was a golden time for young people; although refinery jobs did not make any of our families rich, they allowed us to live in comfort. Doing without air conditioning was only a minor annoyance, particularly if we could afford an attic fan. Education was great. Opportunities abounded, and we had probably more than we needed. A majority of citizens took the opportunity to participate in elections in all levels—state, local, federal, and otherwise. City leaders were honored and revered as were our presidents and U.S. senators.

Port Arthur, as well as Jefferson County, benefitted from the unions. Jefferson County had the highest per captita income in the state for many years, largely due to the dedication of most refinery workers, and as a result, their unions brought better working conditions and salaries.

Technology reduced the number of jobs available at our refineries, and the demographics of Port Arthur have changed. Port Arthur is an amazing city with a broad range of aging infrastructure. There is no reason, however, that Port Arthur cannot rebound and once again become a shining light in Southeast Texas. We have all the ingredients for a thriving economy: ample opportunities for young folks, and more natural resources than most. All we need is strong citizen participation and thinking and wise political leadership at our city and county levels. This, however, begins with participation by each of us who would like to see Port Arthur return to its glory of yester years.

I am, of course, saddened when I drive through downtown Port Arthur today. It is crumbling; buildings are deserted. And I think that in all my years in the Texas legislature, representing my constituents, I was also representing a memory of Port Arthur's glory and a hope for its return to glory.

The Answers in Law School

Eventually, I made it out of Port Arthur and my childhood and adolescence and into law school. And like my visits to my grandparents in the country and my memories of Port Arthur, law school stays in my mind. Several of my friends have often said I should record my stories rather than simply write about politics and my views in that category.

Law School Experiences

Law school was a new and wonderful thing. By today's standards, I would not have been accepted into the University of Texas School of Law—or any other law schools. My grade point was well below a B, approximately a high C. Unfortunately, I was able to manage high school without studying, so I didn't. I thought I could do the same thing in college; unfortunately, again, I was wrong. My freshman year I did not do well and was on the border of scholastic probation. My sophomore year I got somewhat better because I began to discover that reading the lessons prior to the professor's lectures would be most helpful.

My first law school exam was a traumatic experience. Having studied hard, I felt confident entering the exam. I thought I had adequately and accurately answered Dean Keeton's tort final. I noticed that I had only filled half of my blue book with answers while everyone else was still writing, some filling up their second blue book in response to the exam. I looked over my answers, felt very satisfied, and confidently left the test area. It took a while for me to return to my apartment on campus where I re-examined the examination, which was contained on a single page. I happened to turn the page over and discovered on the back of the single-page exam was a fourth question which I had not even considered when responding to the exam. I could imagine myself flunking one-fourth of the exam before it was even graded. Rapid heartbeats accompanied my despair. There was still time left in the exam time but very little. I literally ran full speed from my apartment back to the law school where I sought Dean Keeton and explained to him what had happened. Thank God for an understanding professor. Dean Keeton responded to me that he could tell from my answers for the first three questions whether or not I had a good grasp on tort law as taught by him. Ultimately, I received an 81 on the exam which is a very acceptable grade on a law school exam.

In my first year, I was 13th in my class of over 400. After I got the hang of how to study, law school for me was pure enjoyment. You could say I loved law school. I was elected as class officer and was chosen to lead a group called the Law Bachelor's Club. Not only did I enjoy law school, but all extra-curricular activities attached to it.

In a way, the Bachelor Club led me to Beverly Stiegler, later to be my wife of over 60 years. As a club, we would invite sororities to join us on Sunday afternoons for a picnic. We would rent a suitable place and find food and drink (usually a keg of beer). We would then transport the girls to the picnic.

After inviting two sororities at Southwestern University, a small Methodist school near Austin, we discovered that their college rules provided that no female could leave the campus on weekends without a chaperone or escort. In order to accommodate this rule, the Methodist school's administrators requested that the Southwestern sororities furnish us with a list of all the young ladies who intended to attend our picnic. We then matched members of the Bachelor Club with the list of the sorority girls and assigned them to furnish them transport and escort the young ladies. One of my roommates, Lewis Newman, happened to sign up with Beverly. On this particular Sunday, I opted to pitch in a softball tournament rather than attend the picnic. By providence the game was rained out, so I opted to go to the picnic. After a few dances, I asked my roommate what he thought of the pretty blonde he had escorted to the affair. He replied he was not enthused in that he considered her far too tall to suit him. I told him that, as a favor to him, I would gladly furnish her a ride back to her dormitory.

Beverly and I started dating; I soon decided she would be whom I would like to marry. We dated off and on until I completed law school and naval officer candidate school. I am still glad the ball game was rained out. (It must have been God's hand.)

UT had a great intramural sports program, so some of my fellow law students formed a touch football team. We named our team the "Legal Eagles." We were soon joined by Charles Allen Wright, a young professor who taught evidence and procedure. It seemed a good idea, so we complemented Professor Wright with the title of coach of the Legal Eagles. Another professor adopted a team and challenged Professor Wright to a game to determine the school's championship. There was much "trash talk" between the professors, via the students who attended their classes. Soon after, the game was scheduled and was the subject of considerable conversation around the law school. The game was dubbed "the first annual town's hall beer bowl." Someone prepared a wooden trophy with a can of Lone Star affixed to the top and was scheduled to be awarded to the winner of the beer bowl. The beer bowl continues today at the University of Texas Law School.

One member of our team, Buddy Manor, thought it would be possible to get a little inside information on our first law school exam, so he set about a meeting with our coach, Professor Wright. Manor reported back to us that upon entering Professor Wright's office, Professor Wright told him his visit reminded him of a visit that he had earlier when he taught at the Minnesota School of Law. Wright told the story that before the first exam a very beautiful young lady student came to his office and told him in a suggestive manner that she would do anything to receive a good grade in his class. The young lady reemphasized that she would be willing to do anything for a grade. Wright replied to her that if she were ready to do anything, she should go home and study. Manor reported to us that he felt that, after hearing that episode, his visit would not produce any helpful information about the coming exam.

My criminal law class was taught by Judge Stumberg, an older professor who was legendary at the University of Texas School of Law. Judge Stumberg would never give the answer to a question posed by a set of facts he would relate. However, occasionally, there was a quick come-back from one of my fellow students. On one occasion, Judge Stumberg asked the class if there was a way to discern the difference between assault with intent to murder and assault with intent to rape. One wag immediately replied, "By the nature of the weapon used, of course." It certainly got a laugh in the class that day.

There was another memory, thinking back now, of how things have changed. In my class, there were probably only three female members of the class out of about four hundred. Among that class was a spunky lady whose spunky name was Bunky Duncan. Our first professor who taught procedure was Charles Allen Wright, a genius in his own right but, no doubt, a male chauvinist. On the first day of class Professor Wright announced he truly did not believe women should be in the legal profession and that he had never passed a female student in any of his classes. He went on to say he would gladly honor her request for a transfer for a different professor. Of course, Bunky Duncan challenged Professor Wright, and he responded by reading the decision of the New York Supreme Court rendered in the 1800s. The case went on to justify denying admission to a female by quoting all the bad things lawyers had to deal with: murder, rape, robbery, and all the other incestuous things which come to a lawyer's desk. The court ended by saying that it is bad enough that we, the males of our profession, had to deal with these terrible things, let alone expose womanhood to such rigors. Of course, Bunky's immediate response was, "Judge Wright, this is a mid-nineteenth century opinion."

Professor Wright looked at her and solemnly said, "Miss Duncan, I was under the impression the morals of womanhood in America had not declined so greatly in the last 80 years." Bunky did not take him up on his offer to let her transfer, and indeed Professor Wright flunked her in his first course of procedure.

In contracts, the professor's way of teaching was, of course, to call on each of us to answer a legal question posed by one of the cases assigned for the day. In our class was a veteran, John Davis. In this particular instance, John was called on for a knotty question for which he was obviously not prepared. He told the professor that he simply did not know the answer to the question. "Come now, Mr. Davis," said the professor, "Here you are a practicing attorney, and in your office is a potential client with a fist full of money; he poses the same question to you; what are you going to tell him?"

At the time, as in most classes, there was some smart aleck who was always too anxious to answer the questions unanswered by fellow students. In this class, that sort of student was waving his hand vigorously attempting to get the attention of the professor. Student Davis looked around, then looked at the professor and simply said, "I would refer him to the guy over there with his hand up." On another occasion, Judge Wright, the misogynist, was teaching evidence. An axiom of evidence is that a witness could be impeached by pointing out that the witness was guilty of a crime of moral turpitude. Professor Wright asked, "How many believe that, if a witness had been convicted of prostitution, then she could be impeached by pointing out such a conviction?" All in the class agreed with the professor that the offense be admissible except for one fellow near the front. "How many disagree?" asked Professor Wright. The lone student raised his hand. Professor Wright asked, "Why do you disagree that you could not point out prostitution as the kind of offense that would justify impeachment?"

The guy simply responded, "Well, professor, I know a lot of whores who don't lie."

Law school is based on the Socratic method. Pedagogically it is supposed to be more challenging and effective than straight out lecturing. Maybe the reason that it is so appealing is that the wrong answers are often so funny.

Experience in the Navy

After graduating from law school with a slightly better than average grade point average, I was somewhat shocked and amazed that no big firms or governmental agencies rushed to hire me for my legal skills. I was almost as shocked when seeking public office that not everyone really loved me as I had long believed.

After shopping around for law office opportunities and considering the fact that the U.S. government had re-instated the draft, being without a job and not wanting to be a regular GI, I started pursuing the opportunity to join Army, Navy, or Air Force. One of my friends had signed up for Naval Officer Candidate School, so I thought I would give that a try. My inquiry led me to a free ticket from Austin to Houston and an appointment with a group of recruiters interviewing for Naval OCS. I questioned the recruiter about why I could have gotten a direct commission in the Army or Air Force without going to Officer's Candidate School. He assured me that Naval Officer Candidate School was nothing more than sort of a way to get acquainted, a little period of time when I would kind of be taught about how the Navy worked. And he pointed out that the advantage of going through Naval OCS was that I would end up one grade up becoming a lieutenant junior grade, equivalent to first lieutenant in the Army or Air Force. I expressed some doubt about returning to school in that the last math I had was as a sophomore in college and that I wasn't looking too forward to having any more in the Navy. The recruiter assured me again that it was more to just get acquainted with naval traditions and that I wouldn't have to worry about such things as a heavy math load. I should have investigated a little more. In OCS I was confronted with navigation, engineering, gunnery, and seamanship.

After finally being accepted for the August class of 1958, I traveled to Newport, RI, arriving late in the evening. I reported to the officer of the day and was instructed that I would be driven to the bachelor officers' quarters where I would await further orders. Upon arriving, I got ushered to a large apartment in the BOQ with a private bar, luxurious furnishing, and wide-open spaces. I began to think that I had really made a good choice of joining the Navy if this was the kind of quarters that would be my home for the next few months. Unfortunately, early the next morning, I was greeted with a knock on the door and a watchman told me that a bad mistake had been made—they had billeted me in captain's quarters—and that I should immediately grab my stuff and go to some other place, which turned out to be a not-too-fine barracks accommodation.

As it turned out, Naval Officer Candidate School was one of those experiences that I would not trade for a million dollars but that I wouldn't give you four bits to do it over again. I was assigned to "Charlie Company" along with about 130 other recent college graduates. The first thing I learned was that simply having a college degree did not particularly make me all that special in view of the fact that there were one hundred and thirty other guys with the same kind of credentials, all believing, like me, that they were ready to conquer the world. We had some interesting folks in my company and particularly in my section comprised of thirty other sailors. Two of my roommates were business grads; the other was an architect. Naval OCS taught me one thing for sure. I thought that I had learned to study after about two years of college and upon entering law school. I quickly learned in OCS that I was capable of much more than I thought I could while studying in law school. We had several courses: navigation, gunnery, engineering, seamanship, and naval operations. In naval OCS, we in fact covered all the military books covered by Annapolis in four years, only we did it in four months. We would be assigned 50-100 pages on four or five different subjects every evening and be tested on them the next day. While the Army and Marine Corps early training concentrates on toughening you physically, Naval OCS, I believe, stressed stress. In view of the fact that naval assignments would require living aboard ship, in close quarters, Naval OCS taught how to deal with confinement and serious stress.

As an example of how the Navy went about conditioning you to live with stress, we first were ordered to put our rooms in a particular order. We were given an instruction book about how our beds would be made and how our lockers should be accommodated. It didn't take long for our company officer, a twenty-year old chief petty officer come in, to look at the way we had stored stuff in our lockers, and proceeded to trash it out on the floor, saying he was shocked at our sloppy demeanor. None of us had it right. We redid it about three times, looking carefully at the instruction book, and failed to figure out what the chief had found wrong. Eventually, we discovered that our great sin in storing our underwear, towels, and other items of apparel was that we failed to have all folded edges facing outward for the inspecting officer as he appeared to check our lockers.

As a naval officer candidate, I spent my first holiday, Thanksgiving Day, away from home, standing watch as a security guard for sea barracks. The remainder of the time in OCS, we would generally be bound together as a group, marching in quick step to our various classes and being inspected every morning to be sure that we were properly dressed in uniform, cleaned up and ready for the day's assignment.

Following OCS, I was assigned to Naval Justice School in Newport, Rhode Island and was instructed in an intensive program in learning the Uniform Code of Military Justice, adopted in 1951. Thereafter, I requested that I be sent overseas, put on a ship or returned to Texas. I was awarded my third choice by being assigned to the Naval Air Station in Corpus Christi, Texas.

Later, I often jokingly boasted that while I defended Corpus Christi, there was not a single foreign invasion on Corpus Christi.

Upon finally arriving at my duty station, which was to be it for my entire tenure on active duty, I arrived at the Naval Air Station at 7:30 a.m., and at 7:45 I was handed a file and told that at 8:00 I would be assigned as defense counsel in a special court martial. I attended and managed to assist my client being with unauthorized absence with a reasonable sentence of being restricted to base and a small forfeiture part of his salary. Thereafter I went on to participate in about four hundred court martials both general, special, and summary, sometimes prosecuting, sometimes defending. My boss, Commander Beauchamp, who was a fine fella, believed that we should have a taste of both sides, prosecuting for two months, then defending for two months. This experience sort of surprised me about how one's attitude could change depending on what side "one" happened to be representing. Truth was tough, especially for a Navy lawyer.

My time in the Navy was very pleasant. I made good friends. I married after being a bachelor Naval officer in Corpus Christi for about a year and a half. Beverly moved on the base and later acquired a small house in Corpus Christi; and thereafter our first child, Valerie, was born at the naval hospital.

My experience on active duty was made very pleasant by Captain Coffield. Captain Coffield was legal counsel for CNATRA, which is advanced naval training command. He, in fact, was my boss' boss. Captain Coffield and his wife were very neat folks and had no children. Both loved sing-alongs and BBQs and other activities at their home and on South Padre Island. Probably knowing more Baptist Hymns than anyone Captain Coffield had ever met, I quickly became one of his favorites and a regular visitor in his home where he loved to play the organ and sing along. As my term in the Navy was ending, Captain Coffield attempted to persuade me to augment to regular Navy from the reserves. I expressed to him that I had enjoyed my tenure, that I appreciated him very much, but that I could not be assured that I would always have such good bosses as Commander Beauchamp and Captain Coffield. Captain Coffield told me that he was about to be assigned to Rome, Italy and that if I would augment, he would see to it that I would spend the next 3 years in Rome with him under his command. I failed to tell Beverly, who would have delighted to be in Rome, about this particular offer until I had already been discharged from active duty. I knew at the time that I wanted to give myself a try at the private practice of law in my hometown, Port Arthur, Texas (and not Rome) and to maybe even stab at a political career.

Not only was returning to Port Arthur an opportune time in view of the legislative scandal cleanup, but it was still somewhat challenging in that Port Arthur had been and was very divided between union and management. There was no doubt from anyone that I was attached to the union side in view of the fact that my father had been a longtime leader of the Oil Workers' Union, having been president of one of the largest unions in the United States. Just to point out the division that existed when I returned, my wife was met with a surprising amount of push-back from our union footing. Beverly, who has been my greatest asset, both in politics and life, is a very charming, statuesque, model-type lady. I have never known her not to get along with almost anyone. When returning, she wanted to get involved in the community. At the time, the only high-level involvement for women was called the Port Arthur Service League. Port Arthur was too small to be recognized to have a Junior League. In any event, in one conversation, one of the society ladies of Port Arthur expressed to Beverly doubt that she would ever be accepted into Port Arthur's Service League because of her attachment to me and my union friends. Well, just to show how well Miss Beverly can adapt, not only did she get accepted into the Service League, but later became president of it.

Rescuing My Daughter

People assume that a law degree and military duty would carry some dignity. They assume that same dignity in public service. But in those endeavors and just in normal life, I have found dignity to be difficult to maintain.

My children were raised in an old home on Sixth Street in Port Arthur, Texas. It was shaded by live oaks, pecan trees, and flower beds full of beautiful azaleas and camelias. It was a very pleasant, old federal-style house with two stories and a garage apartment in the rear.

When my daughter, Valerie, was a senior, in order to no longer share a bedroom with her younger sister, she requested that we allow her to live in the garage apartment. We reluctantly agreed with certain provisions.

Our deal on her living in the garage apartment was that, if she had a date or went out in the evening, she would return to the house first and then proceed to the garage apartment. I had rigged up an intercom between the house and the apartment on which Valerie would report that she was in safely and then we could relax.

Since she was a senior, she had gone to one of the proms, returned shortly after midnight, and reported to the house before going to the apartment. We had a practice of staying awake until she returned. I was especially tired, and as soon as she checked in and went to the garage apartment, I fell asleep. Before I was asleep good, however, I heard Valerie's voice over the intercom, which I understood her to say, "There is a big boy in here!" Needing no other warning, I leaped from the bed, grabbing my gun, which I kept under the mattress, flinging the mattress topsy-turvy over my wife, descended the stairs, and flew out the back door. At the time, I was dressed only in my jockey shorts. I went out the door so fast that I knocked the back-screen door from its hinges. As I left the house, I screamed, "Valerie, get out of there if you can!" in such a loud voice that I am certain I was overheard by the neighbors as evidenced by the fact that many of their lights began to come on. As I flew up the stairs to the apartment, I found the door unlocked and rushed in, gun in hand, ready to confront the intruder.

As I looked up, however, Valerie was standing there with a funny look on her face. She said, "Daddy, it's only a rat."

Apparently, what caused the call from her was that, as she entered the apartment, she spotted a mouse lurking on top of the shower stall. We had a good laugh, but then I was confronted with how to return in only my jockey shorts with the neighbors beginning to look outdoors to see what brought about all the commotion. I wrapped myself in a blanket and strode back into the house in as dignified a manner as I could possibly muster at the time.

Part II: The House

Off and Running for Office

My time with my obligation to the Naval Reserve was up at the end of 1961. I had accumulated 30 days leave, so I was able to travel from Corpus Christi back to Port Arthur at the end of November to try to locate a place for Beverly and me to reside and get settled in to my partnership with Shelby Long in the old Bluestein Building in downtown Port Arthur. I was only home until late February when I was approached by several community leaders suggesting that I consider a race for the state senate. As I have pointed out previously, after consulting with my friend Roy Harrington, I was convinced that my best political opportunity was seeking a seat in the Texas house. I filed for office in February of 1962.

After I announced in February 1962 that I would be a candidate for state representative, the task before me then was organizing support and figuring out how to run for office. My father had been involved in union politics for many years. He had been president of the largest oil worker union in the country, elected to the city council, and eventually elevated to mayor. Organized labor in Jefferson County, at the time, was a real political force, and African American citizens were highly active in politics, particularly in specific sections in Beaumont and Port Arthur.

My dad had always harbored a desire for me to be in politics, so it was no surprise that upon my return home from the Navy, he was looking for a political opportunity for me. The opportunity soon arrived. Charlie Nacol, an influential businessman in Port Arthur, invited my dad and me to lunch.

At our meeting, Nacol suggested that I run for the state Senate. This was somewhat surprising in that Nacol had always been a loyal patron and supporter of Jep Fuller, our incumbent senator. Nacol went on to opine that mainly because of the recent legislative investigation of corruption in the county that Fuller would have a very difficult time getting re-elected. When I raised the issue of my youth, Nacol pointed out that Allan Shivers, former governor, had won an election as state senator in Jefferson County at age 24.

I have often said that a politician claiming to have been drafted to run probably had only one or two friends suggesting it. The thought of becoming a senator had a similar effect on me as well. I immediately began assessing my chances of winning such an election. One of my first calls was to D. Roy Harrington, incumbent state representative, for whom I had worked in the House. Roy informed me that he had been asked by the area labor unions to run for the Senate. He also revealed for the first time in a while the industrial CIO and craftsman AFL had united in the anticipated support of him for the office. Roy then suggested that I announce for the state representative seat that he then occupied. He pointed out that very few people outside his family knew he was not running again for state representative, and my announcement would not only be a surprise but would give me a head start in the election for that seat.

My dad's insurance partner, a little gentleman named Charlie Lee, assumed the position as my campaign chairman. My dad and Charlie were like Mutt and Jeff in that my father was about 6'2" and Charlie was about 5'4". Charlie was a natural in the position of being campaign manager and was figuratively a little ball of fire.

I learned certain lessons early in my adventure in politics. First of all, it was a shock to suddenly realize that everybody didn't love me. It is a lesson that any neophyte politician will quickly learn. The next lesson I quickly grasped is how large an area Jefferson County encompassed and how many people lived there. At that time there were four state representative slots for Jefferson County's approximately 260,000 people. All the elections for state representatives were carried on not by place, but county wide, which meant we had to traverse the entire county, rural, urban, east, west, north and south. One of the other lessons I learned, fairly early, was just what it took to be a viable candidate. I sought advice from Edgar Berlin, a former state representative from Beaumont, and was literally floored when he told me that I would need about 10,000 bumper strips, 3,000-5,000-yard signs and all the "push cards" that I could possibly afford, all containing the union bug. (The "union bug" was a symbol indicating the work had been done by a union print shop.) The next issue, I came to learn, was that of money. As I have said many times since, quoting former speaker of the U.S. House, "Money is the mother's milk of politics." Having none, I set out trying to obtain some through friends. Fortunately, I began with a $100 contribution from my own father; my second contribution warmed my heart because Mack Hanna, one of the first African American millionaires to have made it big in business in Texas, gave it to me. I also added a great deal of money from a distant cousin, Oscar Wyatt, a Houston millionaire oilman, and my great uncle Marcelle Bryant, who had also made it in West Texas oil and was mayor of San Angelo. In my 1962 campaign for state representative, I spent a total amount of $5,000 in a race, a runoff, and a general election. My last race as a member of the Senate consumed about $500,000.

One reason we were able to run a decent campaign with so little cash is that we were blessed with a plethora of volunteer help. Countless working folks joined our campaign, and together we produced some unique eye-catching strategies to get the message out. Most of our larger signs were 2x4 out of plywood, hand sawed and hand painted in my garage. It was amusing to note that we were so efficient that some of my opponents took great delight in criticizing my "professionally" driven sign campaign during the contest. Another innovative idea that was a real eye-catcher was that we took half a sheet of plywood, painted "Elect Carl Parker State Representative" on both sides of it, and figured out a way, with wires and other equipment, to affix it to the top of my Ford Falcon. The sign was about as long as the Falcon and attracted a great deal of attention wherever I went. One of my friends, who later became a district judge, took great delight in attaching one of my 8' long signs to the top of his Volkswagen Bug. Fortunately, the signs were better accommodated in pickup truck beds, many of which we were to secure and have serve as traveling billboards for my candidacy.

Texas primary elections can be a rough sport. Having your signs torn down is still somewhat common in local elections. In order to combat this problem, Charlie Lee devised a plan. Charlie recruited some of his refinery pals who owned pickup trucks. They would load up the truck with my signs as well as a tall ladder. They would then, with the use of the ladder, place my signs about 15 feet off the ground on utility poles. Few of these were ever torn down. We did, however, following the election, clean up the poles to avoid conflict with the city ordinances and the poles' owners.

The union would furnish no support for anyone not endorsed, primarily because Charlie Lee and my dad had vast experience with the union and had both, on occasion, served on the selection committee. They quickly identified union members most likely to serve on the screening committee. We invited those members to a gathering for refreshments at my home one afternoon and urged them not to endorse me for state representative, but to use their efforts to see that I won the union endorsement. The strategy worked, and even though one of the other candidates was a dues-paying, card-carrying member of the electrician's union, we were successful in persuading the committee that I would be a better candidate for state representative. At that time, the not-so-secret code of the union endorsement was a simple, small card which stated simply "worthy of your support." The printed card had an obvious display of a union bug, showing that it had been printed by a union printer and listed the candidates by office supported by organized labor in the entire Sabine area consisting of Jefferson and Orange Counties. One of the other candidates, a city councilman named Asa Trahan, was a union electrician and was somewhat peeved that he had failed to win the union endorsement. So Asa had fake cards identical to the union endorsement card printed with his name where mine had appeared on the real card.

For most of the campaign, I was fortunate to have an understanding law partner, Shelby Long, who held down the fort while I devoted about 98% of my time to campaigning. We made every sort of meeting that we learned of in which we could meet and greet would-be voters in the county. There were dozens of household coffees held in my honor; there were chambers of commerce meetings, church meetings, socials, rallies, other candidates' rallies (which we would crash), office buildings, bowling alleys, and most of all plant gates. Plant gates were very popular, and we would usually be accompanied by union officials helping to pass out the push cards and urging their members to vote for the union endorsed candidates. At the time, Gulf Oil employed 3,000-4,000 workers, Texaco, approximately 5,000.

The first opportunity that I was given to speak to a group on behalf of my candidacy occurred in the fellowship hall of our Lady of Guadalupe Church, located in the 100 block of Fifteenth Street in Port Arthur, Texas. This happened to be almost directly across the street from the old house in which I was born. I viewed this as a great omen for my initial success as a Port Arthur politician.

One of the hardest things during the campaign was being mindful to stay disconnected from either of the two sides warring over the cleanup of Jefferson County. Though labor had endorsed me, there was a serious split among the labor leaders. There was a splinter group of labor leaders who had taken sides with the so-called cleanup group who called themselves the UCLE—United Citizens for Legal Ethics. Among these was a labor leader named Harry Hubbard, who later became president of the state AFL-CIO. I managed to walk the tightrope, remaining free of being too tied to either side of that issue.

My opponents quickly took up and published criticism that I was too young and inexperienced to really be an effective voice in Austin for the people of the county. In order to offset criticism about being too young, I adopted and put on my push cards my motto; under my picture I put "A young man with old fashioned principles."

My crewcut, which I displayed on my push cards, even caused a little distraction. I recall one older gentleman who confronted me about my appearance telling me that he had a problem with me. When I asked what it was, he said that he couldn't figure out why a free man would cut his hair like a convict. Fortunately, it became clear to me that he had made the remark in jest and ended up being one of my better supporters. My responses were successful. The issue of my age fairly quickly faded from view.

Among the earlier appearances with the other candidates at candidate forums was one that occurred at the Knights of Columbus Hall in downtown Port Arthur. Among those invited to the KC's political forum was 'Jep' Fuller, the then incumbent state senator. Fuller was being opposed by a former state representative W.T. Oliver. The history of Fuller and Oliver had unraveled recently. Oliver had, at his election two years earlier, been probably saved from defeat by interference of the then incumbent and unopposed State Senator Fuller who travelled far and wide to seek conservative support for Oliver. And now, lo and behold, Oliver, because of Fuller's recent drop in popularity, was seeking to oust him from his Senate seat. Fuller was also being opposed at the time, as I have noted, by State Representative D. Roy Harrington. Neither Harrington nor Oliver had been invited to the forum, but Fuller rose and addressed the Knights of Columbus thus: "You all know me; you know that I always say what I think. Some of you have been for me, some against me. Roy Harrington is seeking my seat and Labor thinks he can win, and if he can, so be it. However, if you choose to not vote for me, please don't vote for that other son of a bitch. I feel about him as I am sure Jesus felt about Judas Iscariot; both were backstabbers."

Some grudges last for years. I recall in one of my senate races that I was opposed by Oliver. But I learned that Fuller, who at the time was in the last stages of terminal cancer, had someone take him to a group of his former business supporters to urge them to support me.

At a particular meeting of the National Maritime Union, as I began my speech, I readily noticed some of the mariners had made a celebration out of their meeting, imbibing a few alcoholic spirits to get them loosened and warmed up for the union meeting. As I was beginning my would-be short speech, one of the fellows who had had quite a bit to drink started yelling that he didn't give a damn

47

about hearing from some politician. He came for a union meeting and didn't want to have to put up with some young whippersnapper telling him what unions ought to do. On a signal by McNerney, the business agent, two union stewards escorted the gentleman from the union hall, applying not just a little force, kicked him out on the street, and shut the door.

A similar occurrence happened at the pipefitters' union, which at the time had a habit of serving liquid refreshments prior to the meetings. I was invited by one of the active union members to make a similar speech. As I started for the stage, one of the "well-oiled" members stood up and said that he objected to having a politician speak at their union hall. He said that it wasn't a political rally; it was a union meeting. Not wanting to be divisive in the middle of a dispute among union members, I quickly volunteered to forgo my speech and just speak to the members individually as they left the meeting. Unfortunately, the fellow who had invited me looked at me and addressed the crowd saying, "By God, I invited you to speak and you will speak and anyone who objects to it will have to whip me to prevent it." Long story short, I went ahead and made the speech and received a great deal of support from the pipefitter's union.

Some people could not understand some strange sources of support that I seemed to have. It seems that an inordinate number of church goers known to be dedicated Pentecostal members were wearing my bumper stickers all over the county. I guess it was fortunate that no one ever figured out that I was being very amply supported by my aunt who was a fifty-year Pentecostal preacher with her own church.

One of the most heartwarming and inspirational occasions during that election took place on Election Day. As I was making the rounds to the various polling places, some of which we had obtained volunteers to hand out push cards and urge people to support me, I arrived at Lee School. There at the entrance of Lee was Carl Smith. Mr. Smith was a former union member, turned businessman, who was the owner of a soft ice cream parlor called Zesto where I had worked for him for a couple of years for fifty cents an hour and all the ice cream I could consume. Mr. Smith, on his own, without my knowledge had obtained a box of my push cards and stood at the polling place from opening time at 7:00a.m. until closing time at 7:00p.m.

In the 60s there were several thousand refinery workers in the plants. At the time I ran for office, it was almost mandatory to hand out cards at refinery gates at shift change—I made them all.

I also learned to take full advantage of images. Once, while I was passing out cards at the Beaumont Mobile refinery, a guy was out there handing out samples of chewing tobacco. I never claimed to be the donor of the samples, but I did express hope they would enjoy the tobacco.

The election went off as planned, and we anxiously waited for results at my home. I was terribly disappointed to learn that I did not sweep in on a tremendous swell of votes and defeat both of my opponents without a runoff. All we could do then was to begin to get geared up for a runoff election between me and the fellow named Dave Smith. Dave was the current mayor of Groves and was a supervisor at the Gulf Refinery. Pretty much the runoff was a replay of the election activities only shorter, more coffees, more gate meetings, more beating the pavement calling on every organization I could think of in seeking support. Finally, after the runoff, I succeeded in being named the Democratic nominee for state representative by an overwhelming majority of about 4,000 people out of 60,000 votes cast. Little did I know that I would also be engaged in a general election. At the time, being the recipient of the Democratic nomination in Jefferson County was tantamount to election. There had been no announced candidate in the Republican Primary. However, I discovered there had been a Republican nominee named Harold Magnus who received write-ins in the Republican Primary. It was a little strange in view of the fact that Mr. Magnus had received only a few more write-in votes than I had received in the Republican Primary. Therefore, I had to suffer through a general election which was not close and required little, if any, campaigning. I was blessed with an overwhelming majority in the general election and was destined to be sent to Austin.

I was elected along with 60 other first term members of the House of Representatives. Many legislative watchers attributed the large turnover due to the fact that the previous session of the legislature had adopted, after a very bitter fight, the first sales tax for the state of Texas.

Although I had never cast a vote as an elected official of the state of Texas, I was branded immediately as a captive of the liberal labor group. The Texas Association of Business had published a bulletin for all their members giving a rundown on the political leanings of the 60 new members. Beside the name of almost all the other members was a notation about their political philosophy, usually which read "reported to be somewhat conservative, or reported to be leaning liberal," by mine there was no "reported to be," it simply was a labor-liberal.

Little did I know that I was about to embark on a very interesting journey of approximately thirty-two years in the state legislature.

Conqueror of Texas Troubles and Woes

Having won the runoff, being sworn in by the outgoing speaker, Jimmy Turman, while witnessed by my wife with my first child, Valerie, in her arms, I was then ready to conquer all the troubles and woes of the state of Texas. I now tell people, should they have wanted to know something about state government, November of 1962 was when they should have contacted me for the information because it seems at that time, as a twenty-something-year-old, newly elected state representative, I then knew everything that needed knowing about state government, or at least, I thought I did. Little did I suspect that it would take thirty-two years to even begin to figure out state government. I was soon disabused of the notion that I knew how to solve knotty problems with simple solutions. At the time of my first term, the cost of car insurance was a hot issue. My solution was to simply enact a law limiting what companies could charge. Soon after being sworn in, I explained my idea to an older member. He responded to me by pointing out that I could force a limit on price but had no way to force companies to sell to Texans at any price.

It was a constant battle between trucks and railroads while I was a member. Both had multiple lobbyists who were very active in bills opposed or supported by their special interests. Jack Bryan was the primary lobbyist for the truck industry and took great pleasure in rewarding us with a free pass on busses. Bryan would show up in our office early in the beginning of each session delivering us such a pass which I was never able to take advantage of. The railroad, as one of its acts of lobbying, took us all on a chartered train to Tyler, Texas, home of then Speaker Byron Tunnell. The purpose of the trip was supposedly to honor Byron Tunnell when he was to become the new member of the Texas Railroad Commission.

During the previous session, Democratic progressives had managed to elect a speaker, Jimmy Turman. The technique used by Labor and other progressive interest groups was that they would

50

withhold any support, financial or otherwise, until a candidate for the legislature agreed to sign a pledge promising to vote for Jimmy Turman. Unfortunately for the progressive wing of the Democratic Party, they taught the conservative wing a valuable lesson. The conservatives used the same technique to elect Byron Tunnell almost unanimously. Tunnell was a bright veteran of the legislature who dressed very neatly and always wore a white tie. Tunnell was well schooled in legislative procedure and the rules of the House. Although he employed a parliamentarian, he seldom consulted him, pretty much acting as his own parliamentarian. Knowing little about the system, I was advised that I should deliver a pledge card to Tunnell, even though that he was clearly a shoo-in to be the speaker with or without my support. After traveling to Austin and locating Tunnell's office, I walked in expecting to at least get a handshake in return for my pledge card. I was greeted by Tunnell's assistant who, in a very bored manner, told me to just leave the card on the desk, and she would pass it on to Speaker Tunnell. I did so.

But, almost from the beginning of the session, I was pressured to go ahead and sign a second pledge card promising to vote for Tunnell in the next session of the legislature. Being hard headed and somewhat naïve, I refused to do so. As a matter of fact, I argued and eventually introduced a bill based on the fact that freshmen coming to a new session of the legislature had little, if anything, to do with electing their presiding officer. I proposed that giving pledge cards be made illegal and would disqualify anyone from holding office who sought one until at least after the general election to which everyone was elected. Tunnell and his lieutenants made quick work of my proposal making sure that it never even saw the light of day for a committee hearing or any other consideration.

*

At the time, Jefferson County was represented by four state representatives, elected county-wide who ran by place: Rufus Kilpatrick, Jimmie Weldon, and Will Smith, who had served longer than any other House member at that time and was regarded as the dean of the Texas House.

As required by the state's constitution, the first order of business in an opening session of the legislature is for the secretary of state to preside and adopt temporary rules for the session. There was quite a bit of discussion about which rules should be adopted.

Unbeknown to most freshmen, Byron Tunnell, candidate for speaker, and his team were well prepared and offered a motion to adopt, as temporary rules of the 58th, the permanent rules of the 57th. The opposition offered a substitute motion that the temporary rules of the 57th should be adopted as the temporary rules of the 58th. A vote was had and appeared to be fairly close with members voting "Aye" or "Nay." We learned immediately that the symbol for voting was finger raised for Aye, two for Nay. As we voted, it appeared that Jimmie Weldon had voted Aye with those we considered opponents in the issue. Rufus Kilpatrick, one of our veteran members, rushed over to Jimmie and berated him saying, "Jimmie, you're voting with the other side."

Jimmie replied, "How did I know?"

Kilpatrick replied, "They had one finger up."

Weldon looked at him with a puzzled look and said, "Who the hell are they?" Later, we all became aware of signals for voting Aye and Nay.

At the time, I thought that it would be a good idea to get an apartment or cheap room in Austin and be able to have Beverly and Valerie join me in Austin for the 130-day session. But at the time, most voters believed that $400 a month was enough for a part-time job, as they considered service in the state legislature to be. In fact, at that time, constituents expected representatives to be poor. So I soon discarded that plan. First of all, I could not afford to pay the mortgage on our home in Port Arthur, travel expenses, and find an affordable place in Austin. The hassle and disruption to the family by attempting to move the family to Austin on a weekly basis, or bi-weekly basis, was too difficult to fix. Therefore, I joined up with some of my fellow representatives Rufus Kilpatrick, Jimmie Weldon, and the representative from Orange, Clyde Haynes. At the time, you could rent a room at the Stephen F. Austin Hotel for $15.00 a night. The House of Representatives would generally recess Thursday at noon and resume deliberation at noon on the following Mondays. We decided that we could save money by all leaving Southeast Texas about 5:00a.m., drive to Austin and not check in our hotel until Monday afternoon. We could then get by with paying $15.00 Monday, Tuesday, and Wednesday and check out Thursday morning. Joining together with transport would not only save money, but it allowed us to stay closer as a Southeast Texas delegation and discuss matters that were pending in the legislature. Being at the Stephen F. Austin relieved us of worrying about transportation in that the hotel was only a leisurely stroll to the front door of the state capitol.

The first session of the legislature brought many other revelations about how things worked in Austin. At that time, the House of Representatives had no office space. The only accommodation made for having an office as a freshman state representative was a large room on the first floor of the capitol that accommodated a small desk, chair, and one file cabinet for our secretaries.

All of our business was conducted on the floor at our desks and accompanied by an extra chair placed beside us for our secretaries. The appearance did not help the reputation of the House of Representatives in that the casual observer would view what seemed like total disorganization: people eating hamburgers at their desks; a lot of walking around and questionable attention to what was taking place on the podium; and secretaries taking dictation, opening mail, and discussing daily duties with each representative.

The hiring process was somewhat interesting in that an unusual array of attractive women seemed to be gathered a day or two before the opening of the session. They lined the walls of the House of Representatives, seeking the temporary job provided by the session. The allowance for help allowed us to employ one secretary for the duration of the session and 30 days thereafter. None following that. Additionally we were permitted an allowance to employ a part-time person such as a gofer or assistant to the secretary.

During the hiring process, I was approached by a lady appearing to be in her late 50s who walked up to my desk, threw her mink coat over the secretary's chair, and told me that she thought I was probably looking for a younger female to be my secretary. I disabused her of that notion pretty quickly and told her that I was mainly interested in someone who knew what the heck they were doing. Looking at her resume, I found that she was married to a well-to-do businessman in downtown Austin and had worked two or three sessions before and was a very capable secretary, not only an expert typist, but had knowledge of shorthand and working knowledge of how the House of Representatives worked. Another asset to assist us in our duties as state representative was the telephone credit card we were presented.

At the time, you could not make a phone call from your desk on the House floor. In the rear of the chamber was a large hallway, lined on one side by old fashioned telephone booths. These ladies answered the calls from constituents and then wrote a message of the call for the representative. In the event we needed to place a call using our credit card, the same ladies would place the call and then summon us to talk to the person to whom we had placed the call. The ladies were known as the "telephone girls."

Keep Your Friends Close. . .

Another valuable lesson that I learned the hard way in my very first term was to be wary of even friends when it came to obtaining credit for your work. I had always felt that Port Arthur was in need of a Port Authority. Although Port Arthur shipped tons, ranking in the top ten ports in the United States, the shipments were mainly from our oil refineries. The Chamber of Commerce handled the paperwork for shipments in and out of the port facilities run by our refineries. A representative introduced a bill creating the Port of Port Arthur. Not having much experience on drafting legislation, I chose to plagiarize the language contained in the legislation authorizing the Port of Beaumont. For convenience, rather than trying to ferret out some other boundaries, I simply used the boundaries of the Port Arthur Independent School District for the taxing bounds of the Port of Port Arthur. Legislation required an enabling vote of the people authorizing the tax and district. I sought to obtain the cooperation of my friend for whom I had worked, Senator D. Roy Harrington. I carried him a copy of the bill and informed him that I was introducing it in the House. At the time and since, it is almost effortless to pass a local bill through the Texas Senate. It can be done very swiftly. The next thing I knew, I received a report from my senator that he had already passed the bill creating the Port of Port Arthur. When I obtained a copy of the bill passed by the Senate, it was the bill I had drafted by hand on legal tablet, but the designation "H.B.," for the House bill, was crossed through and "S.B." was simply put in its place. Although I was pleased that the legislation, which I later passed through the House in the form of the Senate bill, created what had originally been my idea, it was not necessarily a winner politically. The Port of Port Arthur was established after the vote of the people. I attended a ceremony where the initial members of the Port Commission appeared to break ground in a commemoration ceremony for our new port. Not only did I not get credit for having passed the bill, I was not even asked to participate in the ground-breaking or have a presence on the dais for the speeches commemorating our new development in my home town.

The Exam Before the Lesson: Charlie Wilson

There is a saying that experience is a great teacher. However, it is the only teacher that gives the exam first and then the lesson. Charlie Wilson, who is now remembered as a master politician and legislative strategist, learned this early in his career in the Texas House of Representatives.

Charlie was a great pal of mine, as well as a great political ally. We served together for several years in the Texas House of Representatives before Charlie went to the Senate. We continued our friendship as I represented the nation of Liberia, and although I did not gather enough notoriety to justify a movie, Charlie assisted me in tripling the United States' aid to the nation of Liberia. Liberia was key to American foreign policy, being our most friendly nation in West Africa. It was also the location for the Voice of America for that quadrant of the world.

Charlie was a pupil in the school of experience early on as a new member of the House of Representatives. 1961 was a seat-change year for Texas government. It was the first year Texas ever adopted a sales tax. The issue was as hot as an issue can ever get in a legislative body.

Liberals condemned the sales tax as regressive, overburdensome on the poor and middle class, and basically an unfair tax on the people. The governor attempted several vetoes, and the issue faced a severely divided House of Representatives where the legislation had to originate.

Charlie, of course, was among the loyal opposition vying that a sales tax would pass only over their dead, political bodies. After numerous attempts had failed on the floor in a call of Session on the subject, Charlie and his fellow liberals met in caucus and decided the best strategy would be to introduce a tax bill themselves. Traditionally, in the House, the author of a piece of legislation can have the final say on the fate of that bill. Charlie's group reasoned if they were the sponsors of the bill, if things didn't go to suit them, they could simply pull the bill down and live to fight another day on that issue. The bill was successfully ushered out of committee and reached the floor of the House where things took a rather disastrous turn. It seems none of the amendments for the liberal group could pass. The bill came rapidly decorated with all sorts of conservative ideas. The bill went from a bill favored by Wilson and his fellow legislators to one they couldn't stand. Unfortunately, however, the

House broke with tradition, and when Charlie withdrew his support, someone else simply stood up, took over sponsorship of the bill, and passed Texas' first sales tax. Ironically enough, Texas' first sales tax ended up bearing the name of Charlie Wilson of Lufkin, one of its most avid opponents. In later years, Charlie began to see the humor in it and was not so nonplussed when they rightly accused him of being the sponsor of the worst Texas tax measure of several generations.

Even though no one in the legislature had at the time adopted the catchy slogan, "No new taxes," passage of the first sales tax in Texas prompted considerable outrage from voters. As a result, pundits say of the creation of this new tax, forty to sixty new members were elected to the Texas House of Representatives. Governor Daniel, who was governor at the time of its passage, was defeated for re-election by John Connally.

Big Bucks?

While many textbooks have been written about how to pass a bill, how many members there are in the House and Senate, and how they are selected in America, little, if anything, has ever been written about the inner day-to-day workings of our legislatures. Entering the House of Representatives was extremely educational to me as I was attempting to live on the meager salary of $400 a month. While I had noted many uninformed sources of which originally claimed that the legislature enjoyed rich benefits for their service, those sources didn't understand the job. As an example, I once was pilloried by a commentator on a local news station because, as he said, I had received several thousand dollars in benefits in addition to my salary. What he misunderstood was that I received a small allowance in my initial term of the legislature for postage stamps, secretarial help, pens, paper, and other necessary items to function as a state representative. Actually, no representative would receive the cash; it would simply be an allowance upon which you could call to answer the mail from your constituents or perform other functions related to legislation. Unfortunately, in any system, there is room for abuse and the same is true for this system. While I was in the House, scandals broke about one or two members of the legislature who figured out how to enrich themselves by drawing roll after roll of U.S. postage stamps. It got so bad that one state rep was indicted for buying a pickup truck with postage stamps he had drawn from his account in the House of Representatives.

My initial term was burdensome because the state provided secretarial help only during the session and one month afterward. The allowance was for one full-time secretary and one part-time helper. No provision was allowed for a home office, and there was actually not even office space in the capital during our first term. All work was done at my desk during the session and afterward; my law office handled constituent mail, and I paid for service.

Fortunately, some of this was changed beginning with my second session in the House of Representatives. Eventually, the pay increased to $600 a month, but allowance for travel to and from Austin remained the same. We received imbursement for once up and once back home. However, office space was provided during my second term, not as private offices but as cubicles, each shared by two representatives with space for a secretary immediately outside the cubicle. Eventually, thanks in large measure to Bob Bullock who became the Comptroller of the State of Texas, allowance for travel and per diem expenses while in Austin were altered to conform with those level of allowances applied by the IRS nationally.

Also, much later in my service in the House, a small allowance was allowed for office space and for one full-time secretary to assist in answering constituent mail and doing research for legislation. These allowances grew for me as I entered the Senate. In the Senate, we were allowed not only allowance for office space, but allowance for more than one office to cover the wide area of the various senatorial districts. Multiple employees were allowed to provide not only for research, but for service to constituents as well as mail. These provisions have helped greatly in enabling members of the legislature to better serve constituents.

Second Term in the House.

Although I had won my first race by about 4-5,000 votes, at that time, I never had a doubt that I would win. I entered my second race with some fear and trepidation in that W. T. Oliver, well-known, conservative, and reputedly a great campaigner, opposed me. Oliver had given speeches throughout the community in which he imitated Justin Wilson, a comedian, with his Cajun brogue.

As it turned out, my support was much the same as my first try to be elected. I was supported by traditional Democrats, minorities, labor, but a new group came to the fore. Members of Business Women's Group (BPW) came to be among my best supporters. The leader of this group was a little maiden lady from Beaumont named Sonny Lawless. My support from women's groups came from my support for ratification of the equal legal rights amendment. Opposition to this proposal advocated, or alleged, that it would lead to unisex bathrooms and discrimination against women. At the time the law in Texas was still arcane. As an example, married women in Texas at the time in the 60s were in the same category as minors, incompetents, and others incapable of taking care of their own business. As a matter of fact, a married woman could not sell her own property without the permission of her husband. I was one of the leading advocates making several speeches on the floor of the House concerning women's rights.

The ploy among house members was to derail the women's rights legislation because the senator having been responsible for killing the bill the session before was defeated, mainly because of women's votes in his East Texas district. House members who opposed the measure were somewhat fearful that the same fate would befall them should they oppose women. The ploy was to have Representative Bill Heatley, chairman of Appropriations Committee, grab the bill as its sponsor. Representative Heatley was so busy with appropriations that he could not deal with women's rights issues until much later in the session. The plan was to allow it to pass the House but to get it to the Senate too late to be considered.

I attempted to expose this plot through various speeches on the floor. Representative Heatley, however, approached me and threatened to reduce funding for Lamar University unless I shut-up. Being young and brash, instead of shutting up, I made a personal privilege speech on the floor of the House exposing the threat made by Chairman Heatley. I was deluged with letters of support, mainly from the women in my district and elsewhere in the state. A long story short, we finally passed equal rights for women which earned me the fervent support of most businesswomen in Jefferson County. It was not an easy race, and I was fearful throughout.

I also co-sponsored the Consumer Protection Act along with then Senator Lloyd Doggett, now a member of the U.S. Congress. The bill was written by Attorney General John Hill's staff. The Consumer Protection Act is still on the books today. It gives consumers rights of redress for defective goods or services which turned out not to be as promised. I was inspired to be an enthusiastic advocate for the measure recalling a minor crisis as a young father while I was still in the Navy. After our first child was born, Beverly and I saved our pennies enough to buy a new refrigerator. We bought it from Montgomery Ward. Unfortunately, not long after its purchase and a short time after the birth of our first child, the refrigerator stopped. Having a child, we needed to have cold storage. We were forced, not being able to purchase another refrigerator, to rely on a whole kitchen full of picnic coolers where we could store what we needed to store for our new baby. I contacted the Montgomery Ward dealer in Corpus Christi and demanded a usable refrigerator. They responded by having workmen deliver to us one that looked like it had been salvaged from a junk yard. As they plopped it on the floor of our kitchen, a whole host of roaches streamed from the bottom of the refrigerator. I was so insulted that I, on my letter head as a naval legal officer, wrote a complaint to the chairman of the board of Montgomery Ward. Of course, I never got a reply. Remembering this fact, I approached sponsorship of the Consumer Protection Act with gusto. The act provided, and still provides, an orderly system of complaining about defective products and giving the seller or provider of the service for merchandise opportunity to correct the flaw, and if not done within a certain period of time, the consumer or user is entitled to compensatory damages as well as attorney fees. It brought a new opportunity for fairness in consumer goods and services.

During my first re-election, Governor Connally, Speaker Byron Tunnell, and Attorney General Waggner Carr all came to my district favoring W.T. Oliver and endorsed Oliver in a large public gathering in Beaumont. My retort to this power against me was to announce in TV ads and my rare TV appearances that the people of Jefferson County could have a representative of John Connally or could have their own representative. Fortunately for me, at the time Connally had not carried the Democratic Primary race in Jefferson County, having lost to an upcomer named Don Yarbrough.

I was again endorsed by organized labor, which at the time still carried a great deal of weight in the county. Oliver attempted to minimize labor's support by repeatedly alleging that I was bought and paid for by special interests, having been nominated and endorsed by organized labor. This gave me an idea to combat Oliver's allegations. I managed to buy a few spots on television, which at the time were live. Taping was unknown and caused me to enter upon that effort with a great deal of nervousness. On this occasion, however, I was on 15-30 minutes carrying phone books from the city of Port Neches where Oliver resided while he was a state representative. I thumbed through the pages and announced to the audience, "This is a phone book where W.T. Oliver lived as he was serving as state representative. If you search the phone book, you will not find a single telephone number of W. T. Oliver. It seems that Mr. Oliver, who accuses me of being tied to special interests, was, when he was state representative, beholden only to those who had his secret phone number. I ask you then, based on this revelation, who do you think is more beholden to special interests?"

John Connally

In 1962, as I ran for state representative, a governor's race was going on. The Democratic runoff, which would elect a governor in those days, ended up between John Connally, who was very close to Lyndon Johnson, and Don Yarbrough, a young man who had won an oratorial speech contest sponsored by the statewide Jaycees. Yarbrough was extremely eloquent and attracted quite a bit of attention as he traversed the state. However, Connally ended up being elected. Clearly, I, along with labor, supported Don Yarbrough, but I later began to recognize that John Connally was one of the better governors that Texas has ever had. Connally was a great strategist as governor as typified by a couple of his moves. In his address to the legislature, Connally proposed the creation of what was then called a super board. It was a coordinating board designed to see that some uniformity existed between colleges and that various credits for various colleges would be universally accepted. The proposal received a lot of criticism, particularly from faculty members and others who feared that it would, in fact, become a super board and would override decisions of the various boards of regents throughout the state. Connally announced another proposal that the state colleges be divided into two categories. One more liberal arts and the other technical, and that all of one half would fall under the University of Texas Board of Regents; all the technical type colleges would fall under the A&M Board of Regents.

As quickly as he proposed it, I received urging from various constituents to forget about opposing the coordinating board, just make sure Connally's latest proposal failed the legislature. The coordinating board sailed through the legislature and later on was proven not to create the concerns shared by so many. As I observed Connally, I thought him to be reasonable and a good leader. As a matter of fact, we developed, over the course of my first term, a warm relationship that was sometimes productive. I recall leading a delegation of house members to Connally's office to protest the fact that not a single state Department of Public Safety Trooper was of color. As a result of our confrontation with Connally, the first Black highway patrolman was appointed shortly thereafter. My relationship with Connally continued to grow; in fact, later in the course of his politics, I was hired by Connally and Barnes to represent them in several business dealings. My relationship with Connally continued warmly until he chose to abandon the Democratic Party and run for president as a Republican in 1980. This was part of the source of my activity in my organizing and leading the Killer Bees when I was a senator.

Women Dancing in Tents

While I was in the House, I decided that a good ongoing project would be to seek out old, outdated statutes and introduce legislation to repeal them. It was first brought about by the fact that there had been a huge swing in Jefferson County after the scandals and cleanups about enforcing all the laws. Someone discovered that a law passed in the early 1900s made the public use or renting of a pool table illegal. Several pool parlors in Port Arthur and Beaumont and surrounding areas were shut down as a result. I then offered a bill to repeal the statute making pool tables illegal. Strangely enough, some of my super religious friends and sometimes supporters were criticizing me for legalizing pool tables until I pointed out to them that Baylor and several other small Baptist colleges all had pool tables in their student recreation halls. Fortunately, after that, the criticism abated.

Another antiquated law that I discovered was that it was illegal for women to dance in a tent within a certain distance of a public roadway. I got the law repealed. But I never received the thanks I thought that I should have from women. Afterall, I had made it legal for them to dance wherever they wanted.

"The Jewish School Bill," as it came to be known, was an effort that I cite as a reason that almost anyone can have a hand in creating new laws or abolishing old ones. A friend of my daughter, who was the same age, fourteen, complained to me that my daughter was excused for Christmas and Easter holidays but, if she missed school for a Jewish celebration such as Rosh Hashanah, Passover, or others, that she would be charged with an unexcused absence. I, therefore, introduced a bill requiring schools to give approved absences to anyone missing school because of a legitimate religious holiday. It became known as the Jewish School Bill and was sponsored in the Senate by Babe Schwartz. The bill has been expanded since to cover the religious holidays of several other religions.

Barbara Jordan and I teamed up while she was in the Senate and I was still in the House to pass legislation to abolish a legal prohibition against burying people of color in the same cemetery with

61

white people. It was surprising to me that the law had been on the books unchallenged for so many years. This bill sailed through both the House and Senate in the 70s.

While in the House, I was visited by a delegation of baby doctors. They reported to me that they were sick and tired of having to treat infants that were injured in car wrecks and brought to the emergency room. A brief study of the situation revealed just how wrong too many mothers were in how they handled transporting infants and small children in their cars. The most common misconception was feeling that the children were safer being held in the arms of the mother. This, in fact, was one of the worst ways to protect their children, in that a small collision would throw the mother into the dashboard and if the child were in her lap, the child would be seriously injured by being squashed between the mother and dashboard. The bill was introduced several times before passage.

One of my prime opponents was a gentleman who at the time was chairman of the Calendars Committee, and he opposed it on some of the same silly grounds as others. I finally got his attention when I managed to get the bill out of committee and ready for action on the floor by threatening to call a statewide press conference outside the funeral home where the first child had died in a car accident for the lack of an infant seat. That did the trick. He backed off; the bill passed.

It sailed through the Senate with the only exception that children could still ride in the back of pickup trucks. Later on, in another session, I introduced a bill to outlaw hauling children around in trucks. The bill was feverishly opposed by the agricultural lobby and farmers. I suggested a compromise: that it would be alright to haul them in trucks if parents would cover their children with a tarp like they did their valuable produce. The lobbyists and farmers didn't see my humor. Eventually, the bill passed after several teenagers were killed at a highway intersection with a farm to market road in a collision while riding in the back of a pickup truck. One note regarding the hearing held on the infant safety bill is that safety specialists said that requiring infants to be properly secured in safety seats would save probably 600 children's lives just in Texas alone. When the hearing was set, I discovered that Ralph Nader, a leading advocate for safety, was in town. I contacted his agent and asked that he come testify. The response was that Mr. Nader would be glad to testify, but he wanted a $10,000 contribution to his foundation! Needless to say, on a $600 a month salary, I wasn't inclined to find $10,000 for Mr. Nader.

Another incident that helped pass the Infant Car Seat Bill was that my dear friend Kraege Polan's son, Parker Polan (named after me) was involved in a car collision which overturned the vehicle in which he was riding. Luckily, he was secured properly in an infant car seat. About the same week, another accident occurred in my district in which two children were involved, one of whom died, the other was disabled for life because they were not properly secured. All of these events helped gain large support for the measure, which is still on the books, and one piece of legislation of which I am still very proud.

The Junior Bar Association was concerned about the condition of jails throughout the state of Texas. The federal court system had taken over the Texas prisons, and there was concern that the same was likely to happen regarding jails in very poor condition throughout the state. As a result, we commissioned, while I was in the House, a study of jails which resulted in the creation and arming of the state jail commission.

The number of outmoded and antiquated laws I discovered in my quest for cleaning up statutory laws in the state led me to introduce a proposed amendment to the Constitution. While I advocated annual sessions, I also added a provision that the second was shorter and could only be used for budgeting purposes and the repeal of bills. The repeal of bills idea was motivated by my strong belief that most legislators, from Congress to state legislatures, are measured by the number of things they pass, not the number of bills they defeat or take off the books. The more I observe legislative politics, the more convinced I am that I was right in both assumptions. I have not yet received any plaudits for having repealed the law requiring brass spittoons on passenger trains. On the other hand, however, I have received few plaudits for working with Barbara Jordan to repeal the law prohibiting burial of people of color in the same cemetery with white people.

Lobbyists

One of my early revelations as a first term member of the legislature was my introduction to lobbyists. Some were memorable, some were overbearing, and some were better than others. My first recollection was the meeting of Bailey Jones. Bailey was an elderly gentleman with a colorful past as a cowboy, roughneck, and various other occupations. Bailey's method of lobbying was to maintain a huge round table in the restaurant in the Stephen F. Austin Hotel.

Anyone connected with the legislature, other lobbyists, state reps, or senators were more than welcome to Bailey Jones' breakfast table. Bailey once told me that he spent very little time at the capitol. He relied on his philosophy that if a fella ate with him on a regular basis, it would be difficult to vote against him in the legislature.

Not only was Bailey colorful, he was very witty. My best recollection of Bailey was the occasion when I popped in for an early breakfast on my way to the capitol, had a cup of coffee, and started to excuse myself when Bailey asked, "Where are you in such a rush young feller?"

Being a smart-aleck as I was a first term know-it-all member of the legislature, I grinned and replied, "I am going to the capitol to represent the people."

Bailey drily looked at me and said, "Go ahead, that's been tried before."

Probably one of the most successful lobby groups that I came in contact with during my first term was the beer lobby. Not only did they have a very aggressive program, it appeared that it was very successful. Their effort was headed by a former speaker of the house named Homer Leonard. Homer wisely tried to deflect a bad image of an alcoholic beverage by promoting family events. The beer lobby owned a palatial lake property on Lake Austin. Regular picnics were held by inviting not only members of the legislature, but their wives and children. The facility was loaded with fun things, not only for adults, but especially for families. In addition, the lead in the lobby for beer was a fellow named "Buck" Buchannan, a former member of the House of Representatives. Buck would contact each member of the legislature on a regular basis and offer them two of his business cards with a note on the back entitling the recipient to a case of beer. One of the members who approached him each week for several of his cards owned a restaurant and was using Buck as a source of refreshments to be sold and served in his restaurant.

Different lobbyists had different ways of carrying their message to members of the legislature. For example, Phil Gauss, lobbyist for the Texas Trial Lawyers Association, was very personal in his approach. Phil would prepare homemade barbecue which he served in his office, directly across the street from the state capitol. Almost anyone connected with the legislature was welcome to join in and enjoy Gauss' cooking along with an array of different kinds of drinks, many of them alcoholic in nature.

Hank Brown, president of the state AFL-CIO, was effective with many of us in his direct approach to opposing anti-labor bills. Hank depended mainly on members of the various unions from each of our districts who would come and spend a week or two in Austin developing personal relationships while discussing bills they favored or opposed.

The railroads honored us with a free trip on a chartered to Tyler to celebrate the induction of then Speaker Byron Tunnell into his new office as Railroad Commissioner.

My first introduction of the largess of lobby groups was an invited trip to a Texas valley area by the farmers and ranchers of Texas. We were invited to visit a fly factory of all things. At that time, screw worms were a plague, particularly for farmers and ranchers. Screw worm flies will attack an open wound on a horse, cow, or other livestock and infest the wound with worm-like creatures which could eventually lead to the death of the animal. Someone, smarter than all of us, discovered that the screw worm male or female would only mate one time. By capturing the larvae of the screw worm fly and radiating it, they could render screw worms impotent. They would then hatch millions of screw worm flies and release them throughout the areas of Texas where farming and ranching was prevalent. It, in fact, proved successful and eradicated screw worms as a threat to Texas livestock. Unfortunately, the trip wasn't all that pleasant in that our visit to the factory where screw worms were hatched was terribly odorous. The factory was an abandoned airplane hangar near the Mexico border and contained tray after tray of ground horse meat upon which they were seeded with screw worm eggs, thereby hatching them into the larvae which was later radiated.

Other lobby groups that I recall were the Texas Association of Business, and the truckers, who had several lobbyists, opposed always by several lobbyists employed by railroads. AFL CIO had a rag-tag lobby effort manned by volunteers by various locals throughout the state. They were generally under-funded and under-represented, particularly during my first legislative session.

I had a private war with a lobbyist named Jill Devote. Jill represented the Parker Brothers Company, which operated on the coast, selling various products dredged from our bays. Unfortunately, one of the products they seemed to have an appetite for was oyster shells. Parker Brothers seemed not to care whether or not the shell they dredged also contained live oysters, but they were producing tons and tons of shells by raping our bays of this particular seafood. After several tries to curtail such dredging activities, I had the opportunity late one evening while debating a general tax bill in the House of Representatives. I successfully placed on the bill a huge tax per ton of oyster shells. I discovered later at the time that Devote was absent from the capitol that particular evening because he was entertaining a group of his favorite senators at the Astrodome in Houston. I am told that upon receiving the news of what happened Devote almost suffered a heart attack. But as things were during my freshman session, Devote simply turned to the Senate and lieutenant governor and removed my amendment from the bill when it reached the Senate side of the legislature.

I was somewhat shocked during my freshman year by the power of lobbyists in the legislature. Part of my challenge that I assumed, even as a freshman, was to take on special interests represented by the lobby with an occasional success. One of the challenges of my freshman year was the number of bills introduced and laid on my desk for review. During my freshman year there were probably about 4,000 bills introduced, about 1/3 of which were favorably reported from committee. I once jokingly remarked that my freshman year I resolved to read every bill in the legislature; my second term I decided to read only the bills that were favorably reported from committee; and my third term in the legislature, I resolved to read all the bills I introduced. Fortunately, or unfortunately, and primarily due to modern technology, in all probability the number of bills introduced in the legislature today has tripled or quadrupled.

I gradually learned to cope with the landslide of bills, learning which bills to ignore, which bills to concentrate on. Another trick was the procedure required for offering amendments. During my freshman year, any amendment offered required at least three copies of the amendment to be laid on the speaker's desk. In order to enable quick response to bills and the urge to amend, the only method available was a legal tablet with three sheets of carbon paper so that amendments could be scribbled out and carbon copies made at the same time. Today, fifty copies of amendments are required by the House of Representatives, but this task is easily accomplished by computers and copying devices.

Union Organization

One reason I became a lawyer and got into politics was the fact that my father, who was a dedicated union member and active as president and various other offices in organized labor, urged me to get an education and get to where I could be of help to working people.

I kept that in mind and became the author of the first industrial safety bill in Texas. At the time, Texas was and probably still is among the leading states in industrial deaths. Of course, we had a fierce battle over the passage of the industrial safety bill, which was opposed by almost all business lobbyists. Leading the fray was the Texas Association of Business and the Texas Chemical Council. The bill did pass, however. Ironically, about a year later, the OSHA bill was pending in Congress and lo and behold, the lobbyists in Texas who had been so wrought up about my bill for safety, which was dangerous to the business climate in Texas, were boasting that Texas already had an adequate industrial safety bill—my bill. It seems once again lobbyists generally believe that consistency is the hobgoblin of narrow minds. Incidentally, I also carried the bill which increased worker's compensation payments in Texas for the first time in over 15 years.

My second term in the House we were assigned not offices, but booths, temporary walls were supplied in larger rooms in the capitol, and I was assigned to one of those as office space. There was no privacy in that the dividers didn't reach from floor to ceiling, and we were required to share our space with another representative. Ed Harris, from Galveston, and I shared one. We each had a secretary in the outer area. Ed and I were forced to get to know each other quite well.

Another of our suitemates was a state representative from Dallas who felt compelled to introduce legislation to license private investigators and security people. His efforts failed even though there had been a public outcry for some regulation of people calling themselves private investigators. Unfortunately, my friend from Dallas was defeated in the coming election. He contacted me and asked if I would pick up the legislation that he had originally introduced to license private investigators and security people and create an agency to oversee this effort. I did so.

As luck would have it, about the time I assumed authorship of the legislation, a man calling himself a private investigator was hired to operate in a divorce case. As the story unfolded, the so-called private investigator captured the wife in Dallas, transported her to San Antonio, ripped her clothes off, and forced her out on the public roadway completely nude. With abduction and public nudity, the story got a lot of coverage and publicity. The State of Texas could do nothing because private investigators were not licensed, and there was no standard of conduct for those claiming to be private investigators.

Long story short, the legislation passed, giving me a great opportunity to get to know many who were in the security or investigating business. This knowledge served me well. Because of my personal contacts, on at least three occasions, those who opposed my particular politics employed people to spy on me, follow me, or try to find enough dirt on me to make it impossible for me to be re-elected every time I ran for re-election while I was in the House of Representatives.

House Humor

Jumbo Atwell, whose political stance I had never particularly favored, had served twenty years in the House of Representatives and was the dean of the House—the person serving the longest term. Jumbo liked tricks and laughter as much as legislation. On one occasion when he was seeking public office, Jumbo said the reason he had stayed so long in the House of Representatives was that he just did not have the heart for giving up "show biz." His argument to his constituents was that, if he continued to serve, he would continue to cost the taxpayers $400 a month, which was then the salary of the House and Senate. However, if he retired, his retirement would be three or four times that amount. Therefore, they needed to re-elect him in order to economize the cost of sending representatives to Austin.

Once, Jumbo introduced a resolution to honor a particular unit of the U.S. Army. Not wanting to debate the matter, someone made a motion to postpone consideration of that particular resolution until approximately 30 minutes before the session would end several days later. During the discussion and debate on the last night of the legislative session, many of us in an effort to defeat what we considered bad legislation would practice what we called, "chubbing." We would ask frivolous questions, make frivolous statements, continually question those in favor of resolutions, speak against it, and use up all the time we could, hoping that the session would end before the consideration of that particular measure.

Someone discovered that Jumbo's resolution had been postponed to a few minutes before the end of the regular session. Someone raised a point of order that it was time for consideration of that particular resolution. We immediately went to the clerk of the House, only to discover that the resolution was missing. Someone then discovered that Jumbo had retrieved his resolution and immediately retreated to the men's room. No doubt, the resolution met a bad fate: being flushed down the commode in the Texas House of Representatives men's room.

One of the notorious members of the House and one of Jumbo's pals was a state representative from Duvall County in South Texas: Armando Canales. Armando was flashy, often wearing sunglasses and showing off his multiple diamond rings. He sat on the front row on the left-hand side of the House chamber when he showed. Usually when there was a close vote, someone would call to verify the vote. When this took place, generally, the House doors were closed, and members were called on by name to stand and cast their vote. Members not present could not send a substitute to cast their vote. It was not a surprise to any of us that Armando was not there; however, when his name was called, all eyes shifted to Armando's seat where someone sat holding up a newspaper, supposedly reading the latest articles about the House of Representatives. A hand was raised above the paper acknowledging the way he cast his vote. All of a sudden, a representative on our side rushed over and snatched the paper, and there sat Jumbo posing as his friend Armando.

The most famous of Jumbo and Armando's antics occurred when the two of them shared an apartment. Their parties were famous, or infamous, among members of the lobby and some members of the House. On one occasion at their shared apartment, Jumbo and Armando were well into their party late in the evening when the landlord appeared and said that their party was disturbing other tenants. The warning from the landlord had little effect. The party continued equally as loud, if not more so. In a few minutes, the landlord appeared once again, well after midnight, telling Jumbo and others that if they didn't quiet down, he would summon the police. As expected, the party did not quiet down, and the partiers feared that the landlord would call the police. Armando took it on himself to call the Austin police department. Armando reported that he was at that location and that some strange man in a bathrobe and pajamas had appeared at his door and had exposed himself to Armando's wife.

Shortly after, the Austin police arrived and spotted a man traveling from one apartment to Jumbo and Armando's apartment in pajamas and bathrobe. Thinking that he was the pervert who had exposed himself to Armando's wife, they promptly arrested him, paying no heed to his objections claiming to be the apartment manager. Jumbo and Armando, after spending the morning at the House of Representatives, returned to their apartment, only to discover all their belonging were outside their apartment and the landlord's lock on the door.

When Jumbo passed away, having been well noted for his consumption of alcohol, he was laid to rest in the spot he had selected in the state cemetery. Jumbo had selected a spot near the street which was a frequently used thoroughfare in East Austin. Jumbo claimed he had selected that spot so that his fellow winos would honor him by tossing their empty bottles over the fence into the state cemetery alongside his grave.

Another colorful member of the House of Representatives while I was there was my fellow representative from Port Arthur, Jimmy Weldon. Jimmy was well over six-foot, a strapping electrician who had spent a long time at Gulf Oil and was an ardent union member. Jimmy was particularly proud of his Pontiac automobile which we often used to transport ourselves to Austin. Jimmy was so fond of his Pontiac that he kept it spotless. He was so concerned about preserving his vehicle, which was well over 10 years old at the time but looked new, that he would catch rainwater so that he could replenish the water in his battery so as to preserve its length by not having contaminants wear out the battery too early.

Jimmy guarded his Pontiac with great zeal, making sure that everyone understood that it was one of his prized possessions. One morning, as we were approaching the state capitol in Jimmy's Pontiac, we were about to make a right turn into the main entrance of the capitol. Unfortunately for us, a taxicab driver, driving in the parking lane, attempted to pass at the same time we were making a right turn. A small collision occurred wherein the taxicab bumped and made a severe dent in Weldon's Pontiac. Jimmy sped up, curbed the taxicab driver who was not able to stop in time, which resulted in another dent in Jimmy's Pontiac.

Having a short temper and a combative nature, Jimmy leaped from the Pontiac and went around the vehicle, cursing the taxi driver, telling him he was going to pull him out of the cab and administer a whipping. As Jimmy approached the cab, I became painfully aware that the cab driver was probably well over 60. The taxi driver had thick glasses, gripped his steering wheel so tightly that his knuckles were white, and refused to leave the car. Weldon described how he was going to punish the cab driver. Then some fellow walking through the capitol grounds ran up to the passenger side of the cab saying, "Don't worry 'Cabby' I saw the whole thing. You're not at fault."

Weldon reached almost across the cab saying, "Well, I can't whip him, but I will whip you." The guy took off running across the capitol grounds to escape Weldon. Weldon finally calmed down, and I persuaded him to get back into the car so that we could get on our way to the House of Representatives. About the same time all of this was happening, I noted three or four of our fellow members, who were walking to the capitol that morning, approaching from our rear toward the capitol. They were all bent over laughing.

As we gathered in the House that morning, they came to me with a plan to pull a joke on Weldon. At the time, the lobby of the House of Representatives was always staffed by a number of pages along with the receptionist. Persons wanting to visit with members of the House would fill out a request stating that they were waiting in the lobby of the House of Representatives and would appreciate if the particular house member would come to the lobby so they could confer. My friends proceeded to write a note supposedly from some official of the cab company. It stated, "Dear Mr. Weldon, I am Joe so and so with the Checker Cab Company. I understand this morning you threatened one of our drivers. But, if you would like to take up this matter with someone more your size and weight, I am awaiting you in the front lobby of the House of Representatives." Receiving this note, Weldon blew his stack and immediately started out the back door and emerged like an old bull in the bull arena looking for someone to gore. When he saw his several friends along with me bent over in laughter, he did not take it well and began to deliver a refinery hand's union address to us, using some very colorful language. Nonetheless, we had a good laugh on Weldon. He eventually saw the humor in it and took it as a good sport.

Another prank, traditionally played on new members, was the old trick of sending a note via a house page, particularly to house members who had a great opinion of their own style or appearance. One of these was Fred Head. Later on, he was my opponent in the speaker's race. Fred was one of those members who would almost knock you down to get in front of a camera when pictures were being taken. On one occasion, he was preening on the floor of the house when we sent him a note allegedly from a very attractive lady, seated in the gallery. It read, "Dear Representative Head, I have admired you all morning and would dearly love to be able meet you and make your acquaintance. I am seated in the gallery and seated by the lady in the green dress." Head immediately took the bait and raced to the gallery, seated himself beside the most attractive lady in the gallery wearing a red dress—who looked at him like he had lost his mind. Although embarrassing to the recipient of the prank (and to ladies), it was always amusing to those of us who set it up. In retrospect, the recipient might have deserved it; the ladies didn't. I would, if I could, apologize to the ladies.

One of the other common jokes played particularly on newer members was to casually amble by the front microphone, particularly when a member was making their virgin address to other members, and casually say, in a low voice, "Don't look now, but your fly is unzipped." It never failed to get some reaction, some more than others. Fake letters and phony communications allegedly from one's district were also common.

Sometimes humor descended to ridicule the practices of the House of Representatives. A former district attorney, Tom Moore from Waco, was not enamored with the number of congratulatory resolutions that the House would pass, generally without debate and most of the time without study of what was contained therein. On one occasion Tom Moore had offered a resolution which unanimously passed the House, commending by name the gentleman who was later identified as the Boston Strangler. The resolution commended him for his population control efforts.

Early on I developed my own defense against having to take a stand on resolutions that were only intended to embarrass or state a position over which the state legislature had no control. As my defense mechanism, I determined that it was a waste of time for us to pass resolutions attempting to tell Congress how they should vote. It was my position that, if we wanted to influence members of the U.S. Congress, we should make a phone call, visit in person, or just write a personal letter. Therefore, I refused to vote either way on any particular resolution urging Congress on how to vote on issues, especially those that were somewhat sensitive. A good example was early on when school integration was a hot topic, and conservatives dearly wanted many of us to get on record as favoring integration of our schools. Sensitivities were such that, when I first entered the legislature, an East Texas caucus was proposing to close all schools that were integrated by federal order. Another resolution was introduced instructing the secretary of state to reveal the names of anyone belonging to the NAACP. While the resolution would have done little good if passed, and absolutely no good were we to enter into lengthy debate over it, my position which lasted through my entire legislative career was that I refused to vote on any frivolous resolution attempting to direct other elected officials how to vote.

At the time I served, the House of Representatives seemed to be more of a fun place than it is today. When I left office, too many of our legislators seemed to have lost their sense of humor or the ability to laugh at themselves. On the other hand, when I think back, some of that fun scares me.

Neil Caldwell was a fellow member of the House and very frequently my roommate when we attended sessions of the legislature. Neil and I, in order to try to bring a little levity and relieve tension in the House, decided to form a barber shop quartet from members of the House. As we were organizing, we were approached by Curtis Graves, who at the time was the only African American member of the House. Graves insisted we let him join the quartet as our bass on the grounds the quartet needed a little color.

Curtis Graves was the first house member of color since the Reconstruction Era after the Civil War. Curtis was a well-spoken, tall, gangly fellow who was not afraid to stir up trouble given the opportunity. On one occasion I recall a furious debate going on. The front microphone and podium were reserved for those offering or arguing for or against a particular measure. The rear microphone and podium were usually used for parliamentary inquiries or questions that would favor or oppose a particular piece of legislation. At the time the press was relegated to a long table positioned between the two microphones in the center of the House. One particular technique used frequently was guarding the microphone. If you favored the discussion taking place at the front mic, which in the House was limited to not more than 10 minutes, an ally would position him or herself at the back microphone and refuse to relinquish it, saying that you were waiting to ask a question but that you had to be polite and wait until the front speaker was finished. Often the wait lasted until the speaker's time was up, thereby averting having to answer unfriendly questions.

On the day in question, a debate was going on, and Curtis Graves repeatedly attempted to reach the back mic to be heard. Jim Nugent, a big swarthy representative from West Texas, was guarding the microphone for his friend and refused to give it up. Curtis, then in desperation, leaped to the top of the press table, running the course of it, scattering pencils and pads, and scaring the daylights out of the press, screaming, "Mr. Speaker, Mr. Speaker!"

Nugent, undeterred at the time, calmly spoke into the microphone saying, "Mr. Speaker, there is a monkey on the press table." As I said, sometimes the humor drains out.

After the above incident, things quieted down, and we thought the heated discussion was over when my desk mate, a union steel worker from Houston, approached the microphone, grabbed it, and spoke loudly, saying, "Mr. Speaker, you're nothing but a whore!" Silence descended on the House of Representatives, many believing their ears had deceived them. Supporters of the speaker were enraged and began an effort to introduce a resolution censoring my old desk mate. Many of us thought it would not be good public politics to defend a guy calling the speaker names, particularly in public. So, many of us went to him, urging him to at least apologize. He did not receive the encouragement well, saying that he wasn't going to back away from his opinion of the speaker of the House. Finally, he relented somewhat and said, "OK, I will get on the microphone and tell the speaker that I am sorry he's a whore." That is as far as it went and eventually the fervor for censoring a fellow house member went its way without reaching fruition.

My first years were a different time. Those times seem to me now as larger than life. But also, with some moral and emotional jurisprudence added to recalling them, some incidents and people grow smaller in character.

Hearings without Listening

By the time I had sought a third term in the House, I was lucky. No one chose to contest my re-election, and I was able to get well prepared and enjoy a very productive session. The Texas Constitution calls for legislative sessions to start on the second Tuesday in January of each odd numbered year and to last for 140 days. Originally, the sessions were 120 days and the pay was $400 a month. A constitutional amendment allowed increasing the session to 140 days every other year and raising the pay to $600 a month. And there was another tough financial burden. Due to the old constitution, adopted in the 1870s, and a tight construction view of it, members of the legislature only got paid for travel to and from the legislature one time. Of course, when the Constitution was adopted generally members of the legislature would travel by horseback or carriage to Austin and generally stay there throughout the session. In modern times, most members of the legislature would go to and from the capitol on at least a weekly basis, sometimes more often. Nonetheless, the increase in pay from $400 to $600 a month was somewhat helpful. By my third term, I had learned a lot about how the legislature worked and was rewarded with a committee chairmanship by

Speaker Barnes. I became chairman of the Penitentiaries Committee, handling legislation dealing with our state-wide penitentiary system. I had the privilege of touring the state-wide system and being indoctrinated about how it worked from a very qualified prison director, Dr. Beto.

Also, in my two previous sessions, I realized that, if I wanted to become influential in the legislative process, the job would have to be more than nine to five. Committee hearings were a large measure of how much you could get done during a legislative session. Representative Cherry of Waco, who was a government professor at Baylor, wrote an article, "Hearings without Listening," a title that described the committee process in the legislature very accurately.

Due to their "excitement," committee members didn't often attend committee hearings. I learned early on that, if you could stick through a committee hearing, often times the absenteeism would allow you to have a great deal of influence on what was successfully voted from committee. Attendance and listening also allowed legislative swapping of vote, obtaining a reluctant fellow member to vote for your bill in exchange for helping him extract bills from committee. Being a committee chair also allowed you greater insight into how the house was planned to work—and sometimes not work. Most of the time, the speaker would hold a luncheon at least once a week in the speaker's quarters and discuss what problems might be on the horizon, what plans there were for extracting what bills from committee, and which bills the leadership would propose to remain in committees. Additionally, often times as committee chair, you would be chosen by the speaker to sit on a conference committee. The Speaker of the House and the Lieutenant Governor appointed a conference committee when legislation passed one house but is changed by the other house or the amendments are accepted by both houses. A conference committee is usually composed of five members of each house to meet and adjust the differences, thereby really creating the final version of the bill. Some conference committees have innocuous duties, some of great importance such as the committee to adjust the differences in the appropriations bill.

By this time in my legislative tenure, operations on the floor had become more orderly. A member's lounge had been established, eating and drinking on the floor of the house was prohibited, and most side-bar conversations would take place in the members' lounge. Additionally, almost all members of the house by now had either a private office or an office shared by another member. Secretarial help had been extended beyond 30 days after a session which was a great help in communicating with constituents, answering mail, and preparing proposed legislation. Most legislation was not only authored but edited by the Legislative Council. The Council was a body of both the House and the Senate, staffed by profession-als well versed in legislative drafting. It was to be non-partisan, for bills sent to them were to be handled on a confidential basis, not even shared with other members of the legislature. Most contact or fraternization between members and staff of the Legislative Council was strictly prohibited, and for most of my tenure the Legislative Council was chaired by the parliamentarian of the House.

Constitutions

During the next to last term I served in the House, I was faced with a rare event for Texas. We had committed and autho-rized a constitutional convention. Instead of appointing citizens, or delegates, to be elected by the people; in its wisdom, the legislature decided that all 181 members of the legislature would comprise the constitutional convention of 1977. This meant that House members and senators alike would stand on an even basis and proceed to rewrite our state constitution.

Our state's constitution was, and still is, in sore need of modernization. The constitution that was written as a reaction to Reconstruction, which is a reaction against authority, is pretty much still intact today. The exception is that the Texas Constitution by 1977 had already been amended over 100 times. The constitution was full of minutia and outdated provisions and did not apply well to modern day government.

After a somewhat contentious squabble, primarily with members of the Senate, the House out-voted the senators and elected Price Daniel, Jr. as president or presiding officer over the constitu-tional convention.

The constitutional convention presented some unique issues, not the least of which was the fact that the speaker's race, of which I was involved, was ongoing while all of us were gathered in one place—Austin, Texas. The advantage to me, as it turned out, by serving alongside senators in the constitutional convention, I estab-lished warm relationships with many of the senators who held me in good stead. I have said and believe that personal relationships are a key to many contentious issues that members of legislative bodies are faced with—some good, some bad. The good is that it makes it easier if you have a warm relationship with your fellow members of the legislative body. The bad part is that, unfortunately, too often personal relationships outweigh philosophical opinions and that too many legislators vote for the personal relationship rather than valid political reasons. Nonetheless, my experience as a delegate to the constitutional convention was helpful in allowing me to easily assimilate into the august body known as the Texas Senate.

However, I had difficulties. The Constitutional Convention followed the session in which I had announced for speaker. The Convention was fraught with overtures concerning the speaker's race. Probably the most significant thing for me was a burning issue over whether or not to include the language of Texas' so-called, "Right-to-Work Law," in the constitution. It was a big issue with business and labor, especially with labor. I was caught between a rock and a hard place in that it was my fervent belief that the Right-to-Work Law in Texas would never be repealed in our lifetime anyway, but I was getting tremendous criticism from many of my colleagues about voting to include it in the new constitution. Eventually I decided that it was not worth the risk of losing a substantial number of my pledges if I voted to include it. Also, my vote would make little difference anyway. I decided to vote for inclusion of the language in the new constitution as proposed. Unfortunately, it so offended many of my friends in organized labor that several of them contacted me to tell me they would never again support me for any public office.

Unfortunately for Texas and my decisions, when submitted to the people, Texas rejected, by a small margin, the product of the constitutional convention. In my opinion, the Texas leadership's mistake was assuming that Texas citizens were well-informed through the press and other media about what was contained in the proposed new constitution of Texas. Too few Texans were knowledgeable about what was in the existing constitution. Were Texans well vetted in the provisions of our present constitution, I believe that they would have overwhelmingly voted to adopt a new and modern constitution for our state. The updating of the constitution is, in my mind, another lost opportunity for the state.

Fortunately for me, many of them later cooled off and decided to continue supporting me anyway. Probably one reason for this is that the proposed new constitution failed the vote of the people and was never implemented. Sometimes some personal good can come from public bad.

Before getting to my own run for speaker, I might describe some of my examples or predecessors. I thought that I could pull the best from each one and be better than any one of them.

In my first term the speaker of the house was Byron Tunnell. Tunnell was a smartly dressed, no-nonsense, intelligent speaker. Tunnell was an expert in the rules and more or less acted as his own parliamentarian. Tunnell had a team loyal to him that kowtowed to the money lobby, and any bill endorsed by Tunnell was sure to pass. Tunnell rewarded his conservative friends with plum appointments to committees and furnished the rest of us with non-active committees such as those I received my freshman year like Veterans Affairs and Labor. The Labor Committee, for example, was treated to a scrumptious dinner celebration at the end of the session by the business lobby and kept carrying out the tradition of small gifts to committee members; the Texas Manufacturing Association awarded us with transistor radios made in Hong Kong!

My second session really began at the end of my first session. Governor John Connally appointed Byron Tunnell to the Railroad Commission (a paying job) and Tunnell resigned the speakership. I received a call from Hank Brown, president of the Texas Organized Labor, asking me to travel to Austin as quickly as I could to join in an effort to see if we could elect a favorable candidate for speaker. By the time I got to Austin, I was informed that Ben Barnes already had the speakership locked up. Barnes, who was then considered the boy wonder of politics, had gained enough pledges to be speaker in his early twenties. I was instructed then that I may as well go ahead and deliver a pledge to Barnes, which I proceeded to do. Barnes was holding forth in a suite of rooms at the Driscoll Hotel. When I approached about handing him a pledge card, he invited me for a private conversation in an adjoining room. Barnes looked at me and told me, "I could treat you the same way Tunnell did and keep you off any important committees and make it very difficult for you to pass any of your legislation. Please tell me this, what will it take to keep you off my butt during the session from the way you did to quarrel with Tunnell?" I told Barnes that all I wanted was to be his friend, even when we disagreed on legislation and to be treated fairly. He agreed to do so, and I ended up making a seconding speech for his nomination as speaker. The second term Barnes was speaker was even better. He rewarded me with a committee chairmanship, and we became fast friends thereafter.

My fourth session was presided over by Gus Mutscher. Mutscher ruled in a fairly even-handed manner and was, in my opinion, a fairly decent speaker. Unfortunately, Mutscher had very poor judgment when he was tempted to make an illegal bargain. The owner of Sharpstown Bank convinced Mutscher to pass through the legislature a measure that would have created a state version of the Federal Deposit Insurance Corporation to ensure bank deposits. To reward Mutscher for his efforts, it was agreed that he would receive gifted stock which turned out to be a bribe of which Mutscher and his first assistant, Tommy Shannon, were convicted. The conviction of Mutscher in what came to be known as the Sharpstown Scandal resulted in a lot of attention to corrupt practices of our legislature. After removal of Mutscher, Rayford Price was elected before my fourth session was over and began as speaker in my fifth term. Price was a fairly decent fellow, but he was tied too much to the old ways of running the legislature. He was deaf to any proposals for reforms that would have made the system more democratic and open. He was also faced with a new wave of over 1/3 of the House because of the recent scandals.

My sixth term was presided over by Price Daniel, Jr. Many of us had determined toward the end of Rayford Price's term that it was time to implement sunshine laws to bring light to legislative systems. Prior to then, committee hearings could be held in secret, without adequate notice to the public; the public was denied access to many public hearings having allowed quick, uncalled hearings to the floor of the House to which members of the public were denied access. Record votes were not required in all cases, and favoritism offered a heavy hand on the way bills were considered, when and if they were considered. All this led a group of us to determine that it was time for a new speaker with a different attitude and formed the basis of the group supporting Price Daniel, Jr. Price agreed to serve only one term, which brought about my candidacy for speaker.

Running for Speaker

My speaker's race really began with the Sharpstown Scandal. Gus Mutscher, speaker of the House, and his aid Tommy were indicted when Mr. Sharp, a developer in Houston, was attempting to get some special treatment through the legislature. Apparently, Mr. Sharp, who owned a bank, as one of his developments, was having trouble with the federal depository insurance. At the time, and even presently, a bank had a hard time doing business in the world of finance if not insured by the Federal Deposit Insurance Corporation. Mr. Sharp's idea was to create a state agency that could insure deposits in state-chartered banks, feeling that such an agency would be far easier to deal with.

Already a generous contributor to Texas politicians, Mr. Sharp favored the Speaker and his assistant with free stock in the Sharpstown bank, apparently in exchange for pushing through his proposed idea about creating a state agency to insure deposits.

Both Mutscher and his aid were subsequently indicted and convicted of bribery and, of course, he was forced to resign as speaker of the Texas House of Representatives. Following Mutscher's departure, Rayford Price, of Palestine, was elected speaker of the House. The Sharpstown Scandal caused a nationwide focus on the lack of ethics related to the Texas legislature, and reform was the political by-word of the day. Reform called for reapportioning the various legislative districts, and Speaker Rayford Price was paired with another state representative from Troup, Texas, Fred Head. With all the talk of reform in the air, Price Daniel, Jr. announced that he would be a candidate for speaker and that he would be the reform-minded candidate to come in and seriously reform the House of Representatives, providing strong ethics and changing the way business had been conducted. In this particular session, approximately sixty new members were elected to the House of Representatives.

Many of us felt at the time that particularly the House of Representatives had been dominated by lobbyists and that the House had many undemocratic and unfair procedures to be changed. Several of us reform-minded representatives coalesced behind the Daniel campaign, including Neal Caldwell, Bill Bass, and John Bigham, and John Hannah. We raised money, button-holed other members, including those seeking office for the first time, and quickly decided that the best way to victory for Daniels was for Fred Head to defeat Rayford Price in their one-on-one election to the House.

Back when he ran against incumbent speaker Rayford Price, with my help, Head raised several thousand dollars, and even though we were reform minded, there were few if any obstacles concerning how you raised money or how to give campaign money to various candidates. Ethics laws had not been passed and at the time, there were very few rules about supporting candidates for the legislature. (I recall on more than one occasion, carrying, literally, a paper sack full of cash money to help improve Head's campaign strategy in East

Texas.) But Head was apparently spending money on his campaign or elsewhere at such a rate that we finally decided that we would have to create a campaign committee for him in East Texas headed by one of our number to control the flow of money to Head and to see that it was spent on the campaign and not for personal expenses. Eventually, Head defeated Price, making the election of Daniel secure. Daniel then swept into office with a large majority which consisted of many new members, approximately 60 who were caught up in the movement to reform the Texas House of Representatives.

Traditionally, speakers' races had been conducted by a technique under which candidates would collect written pledges from the various members, promising to vote for them for speaker. Daniel, in an effort to be different and to give emphasis to his ethical approach to cleaning up the legislature, made two significant promises. First, he promised not to button-hole members for written pledges, and second, he vowed to serve only one term as speaker of the House. Although Daniel would not accept pledges, those of us supporting him were instructed to encourage members, once they committed to vote for Daniel, to make either a public statement or prepare a news release announcing their intention to vote for Daniel as speaker of the House. Daniel's promise to serve only one term as speaker of the House created a huge buzz among various members, including me, giving thought to attempting to succeed him as speaker.

Having been active as a member of the Daniel team, I and several others received better appointments than we had ever received as to the various committee assignments to the House. Neal Caldwell, my roommate, was named chairman of the Appropriations Committee while I was named chairman of the Calendars Committee: two of the top committees of the House. The Calendars Committee was a traffic cop for all legislation. The committee controlled the flow of legislation from being reported favorably from substantive committees to be voted on by the entire House. Previously, a system had been employed, for many years, whereby bills were eligible to be voted on on the floor of the House in the order they were assigned as they were introduced. The main problem with this system is that some bills, critical and truly needed to be passed, had very high numbers, and late in the session, wound up in a long line before they could even be considered by the entire House.. The Calendars Committee was designed so that bills were given a category of major state bills, local bills, or just general calendar bills. It was very critical to anyone's bill that it receive favorable consideration by the Calendar's Committee.

Daniel was so truly concerned with projecting an image of a reformer that he was very reluctant to pressure members of the House to vote for his various pet issues. So it fell to me, as chair of the Calendars Committee, to be an enforcer for Daniel. Hardly anyone in the House at the time would want to get cross-ways with the chair of the committee that controlled the fate of his bill. Therefore, Daniel repeatedly called on me to round up votes necessary for some of his more controversial bills.

I took advantage of the situation. Many reform measures passed creating a great deal of openness in the legislative process. As an example, we abolished the practice of Jim Hogg Meetings. The rules of the House indicated that bills were only to be considered in public committee hearings, which were open to the public and press and could not be in closed sessions. For bills that were particularly dear to the speaker and his team, committee chairs oftentimes would call a meeting at the foot of Jim Hogg—a large painting of Governor Hogg which hung in the House of Representatives. Unanimous consent was generally granted when requested by a committee chair; the committee would gather at the foot of Jim Hogg, inside the chamber which did not allow access to the public. The bill, generally, by a summary vote would sail out of committee and go immediately for consideration for floor action. Several other measures similar to that were enacted under the administration of Daniel, all for the better.

Daniel promised when running that he would only serve one term as speaker; of course this set off a real scramble, or race, to succeed him. As the Speaker Pro Tempore, I was logically next in line. But there were five or six other members of the House interested in being speaker.

Unknown to me at the time, Fred Head had been telling sixty or so new members that he made a deal with Daniel to not run in the event that he was able to defeat the incumbent Rayford Price. But Daniel, according to Head, had vowed to support him as his successor the following session. This was simply not true.

The race looked like it would be between Head and me, who led throughout the race with the greatest number of pledges. Billy Clayton was running a distant third. Clayton had only eight to ten supporters, but they were West Texans, for the most part, and solidly backed fellow West Texan Clayton. Head had the majority of new members, while I enjoyed the support of the majority of veteran members of the House. Buddy Temple of Diboll, Texas was the most prominent and respected supporter on Head's list.

We were working hard to get minor candidates for the House to come on board, and we seemed to be gaining ground. One thing hurtful to my candidacy was the fact that I did not have solid support of the Southeast Texas delegation. All were supportive but hesitated to pledge their support publicly because another member of the delegation, Terry Doyle, a second term House member, whom I had helped get elected, expressed the belief that I was too liberal to be elected speaker. He considered himself a conservative and claimed conservative backing. Doyle could never count three or four votes urging him to be speaker, but it injured my candidacy somewhat. Kraege Polan, who had been on Daniel's staff, resigned from the speaker staff to come on board and help run my campaign for speaker. Polan and Buddy Temple were very close, having worked together to elect Congressman Wilson to the Congress of the United States. Polan reported to me that he had been working hard on Temple and that Temple had grown very tired of some of Head's antics such as wanting, with his election money, to buy billboards promoting him for speaker and future statewide office. Polan reported that Temple was ready to switch allegiance and join our race and felt that he could bring at least four votes with him. At the time, I needed only four or five votes to go over the top and announce having seventy-six supporters for the speaker's race. Although I encouraged Temple to come on board, he deferred because it was an upcoming holiday—Labor Day weekend—and he wanted to be the first to tell Head that he was leaving and that he was bringing the additional votes that we thought it would take to put me over the top. Labor Day cost me the speaker's race governed by the Sharpstown Scandal.

Head got word that Temple was leaving and was so embittered that I had upset his plans to succeed Price Daniel that he expressed the view to many that he would rather have anyone other than me be speaker. When he saw that his team was falling apart, he contacted Billy Clayton and told him that he would pledge Clayton and recommend all of his supporters to join him in that support.

On Labor Day weekend, Clayton gathered his troops in a suite at the Driscoll Hotel in Austin and began to systematically call all the members of the House, telling them that Head had joined his campaign and that it was only a matter of time that he would be in and that they had better get on board now 'cause the train was about to pull out of the station. He had difficulty persuading many because they had pledged to me in writing. Clayton then employed what I considered an ingenious strategy. Clayton would call a member, or have one of his lieutenants call a member, and offer this proposition: "If you could be number seventy-six on Clayton's team, which would put him over the top and virtually be the one vote electing him speaker, would you then join with us." The most frequent answer that they received to that proposition was, "Call me when you have 75 votes." As a result, it turned out that Clayton obtained approximately seven votes by making the seven members believe that they were number 76. Once he got that commitment, he simply released the list of seventy-six. The seven who succumbed to that strategy then were very reluctant to back out of the commitment they made since it appeared that they were on the winning team. At least five of those who were seduced by this ploy had given a written commitment to vote for me for Speaker.

When we learned of Clayton's claim of having 76 votes, I, along with several of my friends and supporters, rushed to Austin to see whether or not we could salvage the speaker's race. Unfortunately, we were not able to do so. One of my strongest supporters was Jimmy Edwards of Conroe. Jimmy was a Vietnam veteran who had lost both legs, but was fitted with artificial limbs which enabled him to navigate fairly well. Jimmy's problem, however, was that negotiating with his artificial legs left him pretty well worn out. Jimmy spent the entire day and evening with me trying to assist in reviving our speaker's race. Late at night, probably about 11 p.m., we finally gave up the effort. Being that Jimmy was worn out, I invited him to come stay at my rented apartment so he would not have to hunt for a hotel room. I shared the apartment with John Bigham from Temple and Charlie Tupper of El Paso. We would share the expenses and John would pay the rent. Unfortunately, when Jimmy and I arrived at the apartment, I was met by a landlord's lock on the door with a note saying the rent was unpaid and that we were locked out until the landlord received payment. On top of just having lost a bitter speaker's race, I now found myself with a guest, locked out of the apartment that I had planned on spending the night in. As Jimmy tiredly flopped down on a set of steps nearby, he looked at me whimsically and said, "Parker, this just hasn't been your day."

Even though it was obvious that Clayton had won the speakership, several members of my team could not bring themselves to vote for Clayton and insisted that I not withdraw my name, even though it was a futile effort. So, just as a protest matter, I was nominated for speaker, a vote was cast, and I received approximately 30 votes for speaker of the House.

Poor Price Daniel Jr., living in his governor and senator father's shadow, was killed by a bad marriage. Daniel and his first wife divorced shortly after he left the House, and with plans to re-enter politics, he married a woman whom he met at a Liberty Dairy Queen. After arguments but still living together, he came home one night in 1981, and Vickie Price shot him with a .22 rifle. The tiny bullet split and one part defied odds and found Daniel's heart. Race horse Harry Haynes defended Vickie and got her acquitted. Then a book and a TV movie appeared about the murder. Price Daniel Jr. became the bad guy in both.

But Clayton turned out to be fair with me, giving me better committee assignments than he gave Head, and he was very cordial to me throughout his term as speaker of the House. I also decided that, with the end of that session, I would have served fourteen years in the house. I decided to go back to practicing law or some other endeavor. About that time, however, I received word that my senator, D. Roy Harrington, was about ready to retire from the Senate himself, which sparked an idea with many of my supporters that I place my name in nomination as Democratic candidate for senator of the Fourth Senatorial District. I was going to need some help to get up on that fence post.

As it turned out, losing the speaker's race, in a way, was a blessing to me. It encouraged me to go ahead and run for the Senate. I thoroughly enjoyed my time in the Senate, and the Senate gave me many opportunities to alter the course of not only my district but the state.

Part III: The Senate

Union Dues

After losing the speaker's race, I decided that after fourteen years in the House, it was time to practice law full time and try to earn a decent living and a decent life. About the time I decided to announce that I would not run for re-election, I began to hear rumors from several of my supporters and friends that my friend D. Roy Harrington was about to retire from the Senate. I consulted with people whom I considered influential in my district such as John Gray (former president of Lamar University), Bill Dickson (architect), and Tom Maes (an investor who had served as my treasurer as well as leading members of the minority community). They all urged me to seek election to succeed Harrington in the Senate. With this encouragement and after verifying that Harrington would not seek re-election, I announced for the Senate. Soon after my announcement my soon-to-be opponent, Chester Slay, announced that he would also seek the Senate seat. Slay had served only one term in the legislature and had very little to show for his one term.

I considered that I had a fair advantage in the race in that for seven terms I had been elected countywide in Jefferson County. I also had numerous friends, particularly labor friends, in Orange County as well and other good contacts in Liberty and Chambers Counties. In Liberty County, Dempsey Henley (who had assisted the Alabama-Coushatta tribe on the edge of Liberty County), the Jenkins family (who were leaders in the rice industry and innovators first using aerial seeding and airplanes in the raising of rice in Chambers County), and the Jackson family (who were well established in Chambers County) were to support me. In Orange, the then mayor as well as Bob Montagne (the person in charge of purchasing at the only hospital in Orange County) were soon to be pivotal in my race for the Senate. Though not a college graduate, Montagne had extraordinary political sense and had hundreds of contacts in the area. H.D. Pate, another lawyer friend, was city attorney for Bridge City, and Clyde Haynes, with whom I had served in the House, still had a great deal of influence in Vidor, Texas.

Armed with this array of support and full of confidence that I could be elected, I proceeded to announce and file in the fourth senatorial district. The district was comprised of Jefferson, Orange, Liberty, Chambers, and the Bolivar Peninsula, which is a part of Galveston County.

I felt as though I had a sufficient record of accomplishments in the House to stand me in good stead. I had been selected as speaker pro tempore, sponsored legislation which created the Jail Standards Commission, was House sponsor of the Consumer Protection Act, carried the legislation to create the Port of Port Arthur as well as having authored the statute itself, had been an advocate and sponsor for the legal rights amendment for women, and sponsored the first Industrial Safety Act of Port Arthur. I had also sponsored the first increase in workers' compensation in decades in the Texas legislature.

I was quickly endorsed or supported by Labor, at least one Hispanic group, and a broad array of African American leaders in all parts of the fourth senatorial district. The race was very contentious in that Mr. Slay adopted a very negative approach in the race, emphasizing not his accomplishments, but attempting to focus on any shortcoming he could dream up about me personally or my legislative programs. But I was ultimately elected.

Carlos Truan of Corpus Christi and I were elected in the same election. So the Senate required that we have a lottery drawing between the two of us to see which of us would be senior. Having lost the draw, I entered the Senate with the least amount of seniority. The bad part of this was that, as the lowest senior member of the Senate, I received the poorest office space.

My office was on the third floor of the state capitol building and consisted of two rooms: a private office and a small office that would barely accommodate my aid and a secretary. There was absolutely no space available in my office, just two chairs in my private office to accommodate visitors or constituents who chose to visit the Senate office.

The small size of my office led me to come in conflict with one old tradition in the Texas Senate: nothing allowed in halls or other space outside the office in the capitol building. I managed to find some chairs, a piece of carpet, and an end table, which I arranged very neatly in the space immediately outside my office. Immediately, Senator Don Adams from Jasper, Texas, who was at the time chair of the Senate Administration, seemed terribly offended and ordered all my seating arrangements to be removed. Eventually, by simply continuing my objection and plea on a regular basis before the entire Senate, I was able to replace the seating arrangement outside my third-floor office. Although we disagreed, Senator Adams and I became fast friends, and we still, occasionally, touch base with each other to discuss old times and our common interests in East Texas.

Senate turnover was such that I was allowed to improve my office location from the third floor to the first floor in only my second term. After being appointed committee chair of the Education Committee and later Economic Development, I was also allowed additional space to staff the committee and additional office space for committee operations. My office space continued to increase slightly and improve until the last office I was assigned was the largest, best office on the Senate side of the capitol. Unfortunately, I moved there shortly before losing the election and only had the benefit of the large office for a short period of time. I evacuated it early so that John Whitmire could occupy the space. Whitmire is now the dean of the Senate and still occupies the office that was once mine.

House Broken

To me, the Senate seemed to be a very nice fit for me after fourteen years in the House. Some joked that I had already been "housebroken" before arriving at the Senate. I already knew many in the upper chamber, having worked with them while I was in the House on conference committees, resolving differences between House and Senate bills.

Also, with my dealings while in the House with members of the Senate, I was fairly familiar with Senate rules. Change in restrictions on debate from the House to the Senate were helpful in employing my experience in giving jury arguments. While the House limited debate, or argument on debate, to 10 minutes, debate in the Senate was unlimited.

The Texas Senate that I entered was truly a deliberative body. There was a spirit of comradery and cooperation, even between Republicans and Democrats. The Senate was composed of 31 members from the various districts of the state. A Texas senator represents more voters than do the U.S. senators from several states.

I had a good relationship with Lieutenant Governor Bill Hobby and received fairly good committee assignments. I was assigned on Beaches, Economic Development, and Intergovernmental Relations as vice-chair, and Intergovernmental Relations sub-committee as chair. I also served on the Jurisprudence Committee and a special committee related to ad valorem taxes. I also was assigned to a special committee dealing with the student loan program.

One of my strategies in the House I found worked well in the Senate. That is simply to try to outlast some members, particularly in committee hearings. Committee hearings often get extremely boring. Frequently, some members of the committee choose to leave early. The more who leave, the more influence you have on the outcome of each bill pending before your committee. Staying with it also works well with the presiding officer of the Senate who gives you credit for attentiveness to your duty as a committee member—even if you struggle to pay attention.

In my fourteen years in the House, I often observed that many of my colleagues would take advantage of committee hearings by inviting numerous constituents or citizens interested in their legislation to testify. Unfortunately, much of the testimony was repetitive giving the committee the "same ol' same ol'" at each committee hearing. Usually, an invited witness would not pass up the opportunity to have their say.

This redundancy and resulting boredom led me, later in my career in the Senate, to adopt what was known as "The Parker Rule." The Parker Rule was simply that those presenting bills who had the fewest witnesses would go first. My theory was that, if sponsors chose to bring numerous witnesses, then their constituents would benefit from all the testimony preceding them. As a result of the Parker Rule, committee hearings over which I presided almost always had the fewest witnesses presenting to any of the committee hearings in the Senate.

My habit of coming early and staying late at committee hearings and working hard along with a very able staff, soon garnered me better committee assignments and a reputation in the Senate as someone who would work hard to pass bills. As a result, as my tenure in the Senate went on, I was requested more and more to carry various bills addressing state problems. I felt productive in that in my 18-year career in the Senate, I passed almost 200 bills as the lead sponsor and probably another 300-400 as co-sponsors with various pieces of legislation.

In 1979, I was appointed to serve on the finance committee as chair of financial institutions, vice-chair of inter-governmental relations, jurisprudence, and jurisprudence sub-committee on civil matters. This committee led to a committee that Lieutenant Governor Hobby allowed me to perform on and that was for the selection of a state artist.

Serving on the juris prudence committee made it a great deal easier to create various courts, as I did, for Jefferson and Chambers Counties.

The creation of new courts was not necessarily an easy task. When I offered legislation to create an additional district court in Jefferson County, incumbent judges initially opposed a new court. At the time, it required almost two years to obtain a jury trial in the district courts of Jefferson County which gave a great deal of power to the incumbent judges. Some offered veiled threats of opposition if I continued with the effort. My response to the incumbent opposition was the promise to station one of my employees at the court house each Friday afternoon and publish a list of district judges who were absent. Strangely enough, after this proposition, opposition from incumbent judges disappeared. A small problem existed with the creation of a district court for Chambers County. Previously, the district judge from Liberty County ran in a district comprised of Liberty and Chambers Counties. Unfortunately, it was difficult to get a timely setting for trial in Chambers County even though the Liberty County judge opposed the creation of a Chambers County court. It was extremely popular with the voters of Chambers County and eventually no one appeared at the committee to oppose creation of a new Chambers County district court.

Lieutenant Governor Hobby was often quoted as saying, "The legislative sessions are all about money, and all else is poetry." I found this to be extremely accurate and was pleased with my appointment on the finance committee. In this position, it made my lot a lot easier to support adequate appropriations to Lamar University which I considered then and still today, the most important institution in Southeast Texas.

Big on Consent, Not So Much on Advice

Early on I learned of rules and customs that empowered members of the Senate more so than members of the House. Senatorial courtesy was one of these empowerments. The Constitution of Texas requires that the governor seek advice and consent of the Senate on gubernatorial appointments. Early on I learned that governors were big on consent, not so big on advice. Nonetheless, being able to vote on gubernatorial appointments is a particularly powerful weapon handed to senators. This is especially true in view of the custom of senatorial courtesy. This is a tradition not contained in the rules of the Senate but honored almost universally in practice. The custom is that, if a senator objects to a particular appointee who dwells in his district, that objection will be honored by all other members of the Senate.

I was critical of the "Two-Thirds Rule" early on, but after serving a short time in the Senate, I came to respect the rule as a feature that encouraged cooperation and respect among senators. The rule is imposed early in any Senate session by introducing what is called a "blocker bill." A blocker bill is usually an innocuous bill that then rests, for the rest of the session, at the top of bills to be considered. The rules of the Senate provided that bills be presented to the whole Senate based on where they appear on the daily calendar. Having a blocker bill atop the calendar requires any other bill to be considered only by suspension of the rules which requires a two-thirds vote. Therefore, for the remainder of the Senate session, all bills considered require two-thirds vote of the Senate. The reason it promotes collegiality is that often times a senator realizes that giving his consent to consider a bill, even one he is opposed to, would obligate his fellow senators to do likewise when he is pursuing passage of one of his pet bills. With the Two-Thirds Rule, senators either scratch each other's backs or get nothing done. Unfortunately, in recent times the rule has been amended in order to accommodate wishes of the lieutenant governor.

Another of my discoveries was the fact that the lieutenant governor is not actually a member of the Senate, nor does the lieutenant governor have the authority constitutionally to appoint committees, the daily calendar, or anything other than to preside over the Senate and be in line for the governorship when the governor is absent or removed or dies. Senate rules determine the power of the lieutenant governor, which is often cited by the press as being one of the most powerful features of state government. A majority vote of Senate members could change these rules.

Lieutenant Governor Bullock was aware of the office's power. He emphasized the fact that the lieutenant governor is really not a part of the legislature but is, in fact, a part of the executive branch of state government. Bullock would use this to his advantage concerning his income while lieutenant governor of Texas. Unfortunately, in Texas, the lieutenant governor as well as the speaker of the House only receive the same $600 a month as other legislators. Bullock pointed out that he was not a member of the legislature but had left the legislature. He then claimed his legislator retirement, which was more than the $600 a month. Therefore, he not only received his lieutenant governor's salary but his legislative retirement at the same time, enabling him to live comfortably on income from the state of Texas. An interesting story, however, is that I once blocked Bullock from attending the senatorial caucus on the grounds that he was not a senator. Unfortunately for me, Bullock expressed, in no uncertain terms, that he did not appreciate my view of the state's constitution.

Bladder Buster

The filibuster was another weapon bestowed on members of the Senate. The filibuster was possible because of the Senate rule that there is no time limit to debate or offer one's opinion about various pieces of legislation. The filibuster gets somewhat tricky, however, because a senator who chooses to filibuster must adhere to those rules. The most frequent tool for ending a filibuster is to raise a point of order that the filibustering senator is not remaining on subject. Various techniques, however, have been employed to avoid this pitfall when one chose to filibuster. A good example was the filibuster of Don Kennard, a senator from Fort Worth. He chose to filibuster on some innocuous subject and, to stay on subject, he introduced a resolution to name Texans to a particular museum. Kennard's filibuster included an unending list of people he deemed to be distinguished Texans, and as he droned on and on for a record filibustering time, Kennard not only named his would-be honorees of the Texas Museum but also went on and on concerning their lengthy biographies and why they deserved such an honor.

Though not in the rules, other devices were necessary, it seems, for members in the Senate who chose to filibuster. The most common of these was that those preparing to filibuster would change their dress shoes for running shoes, tennis shoes, or other comfortable footwear. Filibustering was unfortunately not so easy for female members of the Senate. One must consider that while filibustering, a filibusterer risked giving up the filibuster if they left their station on the floor or even sat down. To provide for necessary accommodations, male senators, when launching a filibuster, could buy a relief tube much the same as those used by airline pilots to be able to meet their urological needs while not leaving the floor. Female filibusters had no anatomically correct options during my time in the senate.

As a matter of fact, when considering the filibustering senators' need to urinate, one of my constituents, a urologist from Port Arthur, Dr. Petry, wrote an article concerning the urological aspects of the filibuster which was presented in a national American Medical Association publication. Maybe there is need and it is time for female urological aspects of the filibuster. Perhaps the Senate rule requiring those filibustering to hold the floor would be a good idea as a rule change for the U. S. Senate. It would certainly produce fewer filibusters.

Without the use of the relief tube, however, there were occasions when a male member of the Senate was filibustering and had not thought to fit himself with such a device. His allies in the Senate would gather around him for the sake of privacy to allow him to relieve himself. On another occasion, when filibustering, a female senator was granted, as a matter of courtesy, the ability to flee to the "ladies' room" and return without having a point of order raised that she had given up her filibuster. So the Senate practiced some chivalry.

Although, as I learned that senators could be collegial, I also learned that certain senators had disagreements and angst with other senators. But since most were so politically driven, senators could put aside politics to avoid a rift. Unfortunately, this did not apply to some members of the Senate. First among them, was a Senator Walter Mengden from Harris County, Houston, Texas. A law and order candidate, opposed most bills and partisan, Mengden became known as "Mad Dog Mengden." In a joking fashion, Mengden's top aid was labeled as "Mad Dog Mengden's Lead Dog."

Senators need to heed other personal differences when counting votes or seeking allies or co-sponsors of bills. Among them were Babe Schwartz, a Jewish senator from Galveston, Texas, and Bill Moore, known as the "Bull of the Brazos," senator from College Station, Texas. Another was between Senator Patman, former congressman, and Bill Moore. Occasionally their differences even led to what other members of the Senate saw as funny. On one occasion when Moore was attempting to pass a special interest bill, Senator Patman raised an objection. Patman asked if Moore could give him legitimate reasons for having sponsored and attempted to pass the bill. Moore replied to Patman in a sarcastic manner, "I could write you a book about why this bill should be passed."

Quietly, Patman responded to Moore by saying, "Could you just give me a short chapter, please?"

"Bull of the Brazos," Senator Bill Moore, was quite a character whose reputation followed him to the Senate. Legend had it that Moore was being investigated for some serious deed, which might have been criminal. Moore was summoned to the grand jury followed by a host of local press people. As he entered the grand jury chamber, Moore announced to the press people that, if he were considered guilty by the group, he would probably be in the grand jury room for a long time, but if innocent, he would be out in very short order. Moore was in the grand jury probably less than five minutes when he emerged proclaiming his innocence. It was later discovered the reason for his hasty departure from the grand jury was that upon the first question Moore pled the Fifth Amendment against self-incrimination. Moore also had a reputation in the Senate for not thoroughly reading the bills he sponsored. On one occasion when subjected to sharp questioning by his fellow senators, Moore was unable to respond with an adequate answer, and so he simply took the bill, which consisted of numerous pages, and tossed it in the waste basket by his desk.

All Politics Is Local

As I entered the Senate, I remembered two axioms about longevity in politics. One uttered by former U.S. House speaker, Tip O'Neill, was that all politics is local. The other is to establish good personal relationships. Keeping this in mind, aside from numerous bills of statewide import, I was able to establish four or five new courts throughout the fourth senatorial district and establish an untold number of special districts like water districts, sewer districts, etc. while I was in the Senate. All of this became very routine, and staff handled the creation of districts. Such bills were easily passed on the local or consent calendar. A special Senate committee reviews the local and consent calendar and determines if the requests are indeed local in nature. If items are approved, they can be passed in one day in a short amount of time. Thinking back to the House, the local calendar often gave opportunity to those who wanted to make a statement by knocking all the local bills off such calendar. In the House it only required five members to object, and the bill was no longer considered. In the Senate, however, it only took two or three objections and the bill would be removed and either placed on a general calendar or forgotten. So personal relations were very important for me to pass my local concerns.

While in the Senate, I was elected as chair of the Democratic Caucus. I remembered the old adage from a former speaker of the United States House of Representatives that "money is the mother's milk of politics." One of my duties as caucus chair was to raise funds for the re-election of my fellow Democrats. I recall that we used various methods to amass political contributions. One event was a dinner at which Democratic members of the Senate would perform as waiters. It was extremely successful. As I recall, we raised substantially over $100,000 for the Democratic Senatorial Election Fund. Voters must have liked to have their state legislators actually taking their orders.

Personal relationships were extremely important in the Senate, particularly with the lieutenant governor. I was fortunate to have had a previous relationship with both Governor Bill Hobby and Bob Bullock. As a result, I not only received decent committee assignments, but after my first term, I had the privilege of being appointed to the conference committee on appropriations.

Another example of the benefit of personal relationships has to do with Pleasure Island in Port Arthur. Pleasure Island was a narrow strip of land between the intercoastal canal and Sabine Lake. For several years Pleasure Island was owned by the state of Texas. Earlier in my legislative career I was able to make an arrangement through the land commissioner of Texas to have a long-term lease, I believe for 99 years, for Port Arthur to have the lease on the island. Later, it seemed to me the island should be owned by the city of Port Arthur since there were efforts to develop the island. I approached a gentleman with whom I had a good relationship and told him I wanted him to sell Pleasure Island to the city of Port Arthur. We then began discussions on what it was worth. I pointed out to him that it was worth very little to anyone other than Port Arthur because any other buyer would have to deal with the 99-year lease held by the city of Port Arthur. The lease, which in my opinion, and later on his opinion, reduced the value severely. Ultimately, I was able, because of a personal relationship with him, to have him agree to sell the island from the state to Port Arthur for a mere $75,000. Unfortunately, due to lack of adequate leadership on the part of the city council of Port Arthur, the island is still largely under-developed.

A conference committee is formed when the House passes one version of a bill and the Senate passes another. The speaker of the House will appoint five members, the lieutenant governor five members, and the ten will compose the conference committee. The conference committee has a broad range of discretion to adjust the differences in the bill and come up with the final passage. The conference committee on appropriations is one of the most important committees in the entire legislature. As a practical matter, to attain a majority vote in a conference committee, generally, the chairman of the conference committee will make deals with the various members. A youth detention facility to be built shows the power a member of the conference committee can have. The appropriation committees of both houses had appropriated $40 million for a youth facility. The conference committee was going on and reached the point that we needed to come up with a final solution. John Montford, chairman of the committee at the time, came to me and asked what it would take to get my vote for the conference committee report. I told him it was simple. I wanted the $40 million facility to be built in Jefferson County. As quickly as I said it, it became a reality, and ultimately the facility was, in fact, built in Jefferson County. Unfortunately, only a few years after it was built the authorities in Austin abandoned it. It now exists under the ownership of Jefferson County.

While I was serving under Hobby as chairman of the education committee, Hobby saw fit to place me on the finance committee and ultimately the conference committee on finance. Also, he and I felt it important to be in on decisions related to expenditure of tax money in the field of education since education was one of the top priorities and functions of the legislature every two years. Being both on education and finance, I was able to see that Lamar University was adequately funded as well as Port Arthur and Orange. Additionally, because I was the author of a bill to create constitutional funding for colleges and universities outside the A&M and University of Texas systems, I was able to ensure the longevity of Lamar Port Arthur and Orange by including them in the institutions that would share in what is called the HEAF Fund. The HEAF Fund is a constitutional fund to see that some money is constitutionally set aside for all colleges outside the A&M and UT system. Additionally, I was able to expand uses of the Permanent University Fund, which previously had only been divided between Texas A&M and UT, to include all colleges which we placed in either in the A&M system or the UT system. Some of these were UT El Paso, Prairie View A&M, and many others which have benefited greatly since that time.

Another key to success and to ensure a high rate of passage of bills that you sponsor while serving both in the Senate and the House is gaining a reputation for having an able staff and for being dedicated to closely following the legislative process. Frankly, many of my colleagues appeared to be more interested in having a good time while serving in the legislature than keeping their noses to the grindstone and turning out various pieces of legislation to make a better life for their constituents. One of my colleagues, when being criticized for his lack of passing bills, allowed to his constituents that he was simply in the Senate as a watchdog to try to kill bad bills. His strategy must have worked because he was able to survive many terms.

Dealing with lobbyists is another skill which you must master in order to survive for any length of time in the legislature. In my opinion, there are two ways to deal with the lobby, which in the Texas legislature has more than enough strength to influence legislation. One is to be of great assistance to those you agree with and gain their respect. The other is to gain the fear of those who oppose your legislation. How well you get along with the lobbyists working in the state of Texas is usually reflected in your ability to raise funds for re-election.

Members of the Senate, particularly, find ways to avoid open meetings. During my tenure in the Texas Senate, the Senate made a change related to approval or disapproval of gubernatorial appointments. The constitution provides that gubernatorial appointments are subject to the advice and consent of the Texas Senate. As said, I always found that governors are very big on consent, not so on advice as to their appointments. The constitution provides that the only approved closed meetings of the Senate are on the approval or disapproval of the Senate gubernatorial appointments. During my tenure in the Senate, a majority of us decided that it was in the public interest to open these discussions and votes to the general public. That has continued to the present day.

Alligators

Of course, taking care of the local folks is very important to remaining elected. One of the larger state parks is located in Jefferson County in the heart of my old district. I received many complaints that even though it was logical, hunting was not allowed in state parks. I, therefore, carried a bill to legalize hunting in state parks. It passed. This stood me in good stead with sportsmen. Additionally, I was contacted by the owners of the Orange County shooting range. They were hard up for funds and, after my staff's short research, I discovered that shooting range owners or participants could receive federal dollars for gun safety instruction. As a result, I passed such a bill and was rewarded with a lifetime membership in the Orange Gun Club.

After I worked with Parks and Wildlife, that department requested that I give attention to boating safety. There were several bills recommended by Parks and Wildlife Department that I gladly carried. Among them was the BWI bill, boating while intoxicated. Boat wrecks or accidents on Texas lakes were reaching epidemic proportion, and most were related to the consumption of alcohol while pleasure boating.

Another area in which I worked with Parks and Wildlife was the saga of my connection with alligators. I learned that alligators in Texas were about to be on the endangered list while I was in the House. I also learned that alligators are essential to the coastal ecology. Alligators, by nature, in order to hatch their eggs, wallow out ponds in marshy areas, pushing the reeds and vegetation into a heap. The female alligators then lay their eggs on top of the heap they built and then cover them with more vegetation. Afterwards, in order to keep predators such as otters and muskrats from eating the eggs, the female alligator urinates on the pile which causes decomposition and brings heat to the eggs. The holes left by the alligators making the heap oft-times are the only water source in times of drought in marshy areas. Thus we needed to preserve the alligator population. I was also told by many conservationists that it was well-nigh impossible to charge people with illegal alligator hunting although there was a law forbidding it. The reason was that you could not identify from whence an alligator came. When game wardens captured people in possession of dead alligators, the alligator hunters would claim that the alligator came from another state, particularly Louisiana. There was no way to identify whether or not this statement was true.

I had several hunters and outdoorsmen in my area who were seriously concerned about the plight of the alligators; they were so concerned that they would trap alligators and carve their initials into the skin of the gator so that it could later be identified if captured by an illegal hunter. Eventually, I was able to pass through the House of Representatives a bill making it illegal to have in your possession any part of an alligator or the alligator itself. As a result of this legislation, alligators began to thrive. By the time I reached the Senate, alligators had more than survived. They had become so plentiful that there were complaints in part of my district that alligators in areas near bayous or ponds were attacking people's pets. After checking with Parks and Wildlife, I confirmed that alligators had made a huge comeback in that we had done away with the greatest predator of gators—humans! In working with Parks and Wildlife, I introduced legislation in the Senate to allow the hunting of gators. First of all, the hunter had to get a permit, then attend an educational lecture about alligators and dealing with one after capture. As a result, I was invited on an alligator hunt. I snared and killed about a 10-foot alligator, which I later had reduced to a belt and cowboy boots.

Those folks who have never had the responsibility of presiding over or having a hand in legislation do not realize the magnitude and political implications of the game and fish laws. Some of the biggest battles that I witnessed during my time in the legislature concerned commercial fishermen as opposed to sports fishermen in the taking of red fish. In East Texas one could easily be physically assaulted for expressing a view favoring outlawing hunting deer with dogs. In Jefferson and Orange counties, you could expect a large crowd any time there was a discussion of what laws related to shrimping should be.

Hunting with dogs was a particularly emotional issue in East Texas. Many East Texans had for many years had the tradition of hunting deer with dogs. The procedure would be that hunters would station themselves around an area where the dogs would be loosed and shoot the deer if they ran through a clearing nearby. While the hunters insisted that no more deer were being killed by this method than any other method, what they failed to understand was that during hunting season it was also the time for mating. Unfortunately, when dogs would track and chase a female deer, often it would result in the doe losing her fawn. Eventually, we outlawed the method of hunting and with some transplants from Southeast Texas the deer population in wooded areas of East Texas has grown spectacularly.

The same is true of controversy as to shrimping. Many of my constituents either were professional shrimpers or some who shrimped regularly in small boats to supplement their income. There was a constant battle between sports fishermen and commercial fishermen as to whether we should put greater limits on red fish and shrimping. During the campaign I was required to attend numerous meetings of both groups and listen to the arguments in favor or opposition to amendments to the shrimp laws.

I was also proud to offer, successfully, several other bills aimed at protecting the earth. For example, I sponsored a bill requiring cleanup of oil spills and providing penalties for those who failed to do so. Additionally, I learned that one of the great threats to the ecology of Texas were trash tires. Used tires were being dumped here and there all over Texas. A pile of tires will completely ruin land useful for farming or any other purpose. Once tires have remained on a piece of property, they are almost impossible to remove without great expense. As a result, the staff researched what might be done, and I helped to design a bill that was designed to promote the use of tires in various productive ways. As a result, legislation promoted the shredding and grinding of tires making crumb rubber available for the highway department to mix with asphalt. Although such a mixture of paving material is a little more expensive, I am told that it lasts at least twice as long and gives a far better, smoother ride on the state highways. One bill to help the ecology of the nation and to also help Lamar University was a bill in which Lamar University was established as a hazardous waste center. This promoted Lamar to be able to join with several other universities in the effort to study how solid waste could become useable instead of a problem. This resulted in grants for research at Lamar.

I even roamed into the field of health in my efforts while in the Senate. My top office administrator, Dora McDonald, enrolled in the LBJ School and received her master's degree. While there, Dora wrote a paper on diabetes. I attended some meetings with people concerned with diabetes prior to this, but the paper written by Dora encouraged me to see what could be done. The study revealed that Texas was a hotbed of diabetes, particularly among Hispanic citizens. Hispanics were five times more likely to succumb to diabetes than any other ethnic group. Examining what the state's health department was doing, I discovered that about half the state's diabetic problem could be solved by proper diet and early identification of the symptoms. I argued to my fellow senators that billions of dollars were flowing out of the state treasury to treat the ill-effects of diabetics: kidney disease, blindness, and other ailments, most of which were eventually fatal. Funds for these illnesses were needlessly flowing out of the treasury. I checked with the health department and was able to argue to the Senate that the state department was doing little or nothing. I humorously said that when a person shows up with diabetes for help at a state health facility, he would be asked, "Are you blind? Do you need kidney dialysis? Are you passing out? If not, come back when you get worse. We have a program for you." We, therefore, passed legislation to create a diabetic council requiring us to set aside money destined to the health department to be used on treatment and screening of diabetics in the state. Unfortunately, shortly after I left the Senate, the bureaucrats took over and melted this appropriation into the state health department, and it is questionable now whether or not the health department is adequately addressing prevention or lessening the effects of diabetes in Texas.

While dealing with procedural matters and tough votes in the legislature, almost all members developed some protective system or habits. Early on in my legislative career, I was challenged by some of my colleagues who would, in fact, offer resolutions to Congress. For example, while I was in the House, a resolution appeared to stop the integration of schools. I knew that the resolution was an exercise in futility and that I did not particularly want to vote on it. At that point, I announced that resolutions to Congress were a waste of time and that, if we had recommendations for our congressman as to how he or she was to vote, it would take a simple phone call, letter, or visit. Therefore, I would not waste my time nor the time of my fellow legislators debating such worthless issues.

This practice held me in good stead my entire career in that I was able to avoid wasting time or political capital on taking a stand on resolutions to Congress. On one occasion, however, I was able to substitute a way to influence Congress without succumbing to going back on my practice of not supporting resolutions. There was a particular shortage of hydrocarbons in the world, and many of us felt that Congress was not adequately addressing our plight. I introduced a bill, not to send a resolution to Congress, but a bill authorizing the dispatch of a special appointed committee of the legislature to travel to Washington and make our wishes known to the Texas senators and congressmen. The bill turned out to be a success. We were well received in Washington and resulted in favorable action on the part of Texas congressional representatives. Most politicians, including myself, sometimes find it necessary to engage in a bitter demagoguery, particularly when you see an opening to take credit for something favored by the general public. The same was true in this episode concerning taking a delegation to the United States Congress to decry problems related to the fuel shortages. Naturally, I felt compelled to take some credit for shortening long lines at service stations that were prevalent and a source of irritation to most of my constituents. To voters, understanding fuel shortages is tough, but waiting in line is readily apparent.

Letter from a Constituent

While I received hundreds, if not thousands of letters in my 32 years of serving in the legislature, there is still one that stands out related to a bill allowing wives to legitimately kill their husbands' lovers. For many years there was a law on the books in Texas making it legal for a husband to slay his wife's paramour if caught *in para dilecto* (a compromising situation). Women's groups believed this archaic law clearly demonstrated the plight of women in Texas. A legislator from Texarkana introduced a bill granting wives equal privileges. The hearing was lively and somewhat amusing since many of the committee members made jokes about a bill authorizing mass carnage and was well attended by the press. Only a few days after the hearing, I received a letter from Beaumont, Texas. The letter read as follows:

> *Dear Representative Parker, I read in the* Enterprise *that you are a member of the committee which allows wives to kill the husbands' girlfriends. For God's sake, do not let this law pass or my wife will kill the woman I love.*

A week or so later I was in the district domestic court and related the contents of this letter to Judge Ethridge Wright who presided over the Court of Domestic Relations in the county. Judge Wright asked for the name of the author of the letter, and when it was revealed, he looked at me and said, "He's serious, his wife would kill her." Apparently, the story behind the story is that the gentleman who wrote me the letter realized early on he had entered into a bad marriage. He deserted his new bride and took up with another lady. He lived with the lady for several years and had children with her. The gentleman attempted on numerous occasions to divorce his wife but was unsuccessful. At the time, Texas law had a complete defense to divorce. It was called "recrimination." In other words, a person sued for divorce could successfully defend on the grounds that the one seeking divorce had engaged in conduct equally as bad as alleged in the divorce petition. The spouse in this case would always use this defense citing the adulterous conduct of her husband, therefore, denying him a divorce. Apparently, the litigation between the two had gone on for several years.

Texas Monthly

I suspect that due to my efforts to preserve the environment, Lieutenant Governor Bullock tapped me for a serious project designed to make a more efficient government. At that time, there were five separate agencies that dealt with water, air, soil, and other environmental matters. The proposal which I sponsored success-fully was the creation of the TCEQ, Texas Committee on Environmental Quality.

Prior to enactment of this bill, those wanting to engage in start-up industrial projects were required to seek permits from multiple state agencies. Creating the TCEQ allowed and still allows developers to seek a permit at one agency covering the entire spectrum of regulation for new industry. It also oversees and is able to levy fines for polluting our air, water, and land.

Having successfully passed that, along with my efforts for education reform, I believe earned me the honor of being selected by *Texas Monthly Magazine* as one of the 10 best legislators. Unfortunately, with a series of conservative governors, appointments have been made to the TCEQ of former employees of various industries or special interest lobby groups which are very reluctant to burden businesses and industry with the onus of looking after our environment.

Ironically enough it was a pleasure receiving the honor from *Texas Monthly,* but I have to recall the creation of the magazine's practice of naming the ten best and ten worst members of the legislature. Several years previously, when I was still a member of the House, several of us were well acquainted with writers and reporters for *Texas Monthly.* On one evening, while we were gathered at a mutual friend's home in Austin, the selection of the ten best and ten worst legislators came up. The more that our minds were stimulated by intoxicating drinks, the better the idea sounded. We launched into almost an all-evening discussion of those who should be named in each category. The session lasted until the wee hours of the morning, but resulted in the very first *Texas Monthly* selection of the ten best and ten worst. I was modest enough at the time to not advocate listing me in either category.

Killer Bees

Lieutenant Governor Hobby has said more than once since he left office that one of the mistakes he made as presiding officer of the Senate was attempting to do away with the "Two-Thirds Rule" and assume sole power to place measures up for a vote without a vote of the Senate. The Two-Thirds Rule had been honored in the Senate for about 50 years. As I have said in the past, I once thought it was very undemocratic, but later came to believe, after serving for a while in the Senate, that it served a great purpose in encouraging collegiality among members in the Senate and bi-partisanship concerning important issues for the state. The Two-Thirds Rule was usually reasonably applied, in that most of the time fellow senators, even if they were opposed to your bill, would vote to allow it to be debated and reach the floor because of knowing that later on they would need the same favor from other senators.

Hobby, who had in the past been a parliamentarian for the Senate, had studied the rules and became convinced that as lieutenant governor he had authority to place measures before us without honoring the Two-Thirds Rule. This measure accounted for the Killer Bees episode. Hobby, to his credit, notified the senate in advance that he intended to place a bill designed to help John Connally run for president on the Senate calendar.

In order to help a favorite son, John Connally, who had announced for the 1980 Republican presidential primary race, Hobby suggested a special Texas primary election that would, of course, give Connally a boost in the Republican primary.

Several of us gathered in my office on the evening before the matter was to be presented to us on the floor and discussed what, if anything, we could do to block this particular move by our lieutenant governor. Finally, most of our group decided there was really nothing we could do but submit. At the time I had an idea and announced to the group that, if they would follow my lead, I had a way that we could thwart the lieutenant governor's ambition on this matter. I suggested that we break a quorum. Dissenting voices in the group chimed in that such a move would never work. Many times both in the House and Senate there had been efforts to break a quorum to defeat a particular measure. In almost every event, the quorum was restored by someone giving up or being captured by the appropriate authorities.

I must note here that, when a quorum is lacking, in either the House or the Senate, one of the few motions that can be adopted by the minority remaining is to place a "call" on the House or the Senate. When a call is placed on the body, the members present are not allowed to leave and law enforcement agencies are instructed to arrest the absent members and return them to the appropriate body.

For these reasons, my fellow senators at the time thought we could never be successful. I laid out my plan by telling the group that I would locate a place for us to gather the next morning, but I would only share its location a few minutes before we were to meet. I passed out the responsibility to three other members. Each was to call two or three members to notify them as to where we were to meet and we would meet almost instantaneously. To this end, I attempted to obtain a suite of rooms in one of the local motels, which, fortunately for our success, I was unable to do so in that there were several conventions in town and no hotel or motel space was available. My secretary Dora McDonald, however, offered to prepare breakfast for us all; therefore, I sent out the word about thirty minutes before we were to meet that all were to gather at the McDonald home, about two miles from the state capitol. One of our members, however, was in Oklahoma on a business trip and another was at a religious retreat in Mexico. When I contacted them, they promised to remain where they were, out of reach for Texas authorities seeking us due to the quorum call.

We did, in fact, gather for breakfast at about the time the Senate was due to convene. I made a call to the lieutenant governor's office. The call was answered, not by the lieutenant governor, but by his friend, the secretary of state. I asked him to convey to the lieutenant governor that if he would give up the foolishness about having two primary elections to help Connally, we would return in the closing days of the Senate and attend to the business we considered more important. He put me on hold and returned in a few minutes telling me that he had passed on my message to Lieutenant Governor Hobby, who responded that he was not going to do so because he could hold out longer than we could. With this incentive, it was easy to persuade my fellow senators to remain absent from the session.

Following my conversation with the secretary of state, we began to mobilize our efforts to stay gone and avoid capture. First, with the assistance of the McDonald family, we had all of our cars ferried to the Austin airport in hopes that it would make the authorities believe that we had flown out of Texas. Then the McDonalds offered us the use of a utility-type apartment that had been created in their garage as a place for their daughter who was a freshman in college. It was a one-bedroom affair with a bath and amply furnished for one, but not convenient for the number of grown males that were destined to occupy the space longer than we had planned. We, however, retired to the efficiency apartment and shortly after were able to listen to the broadcast that was being made on an FM station from the floor of the Texas Senate for entertainment.

Most of the speeches were by conservative members of the Senate ranting on and on about how we were guilty of dereliction of our duty, not wanting to serve the people. We were selfish and on and on. About this time, Hobby had deemed us to simply be a bunch of Killer Bees wanting to kill or sting everything in sight for which we disagreed. The Killer Bee moniker became a great favorite for discussion with the news media. Eventually the national TV networks picked up the term. Hobby once was lamenting that he had in fact given us the catchy phrase name of Killer Bees when one of his friends told him that it was his fault. "Why," asked Hobby, "is it my fault?" The friend told Hobby that had he simply called us a bunch of "assholes," no one would have remembered.

Most of the time in our exile, our discussions were about Senate rules. We worried about how long we needed to be gone to thwart the passage of the bill we disfavored. Friends of the McDonald's brought us food on a regular basis, along with an ample supply of wine which helped alleviate our boredom to some degree.

Numerous amusing things occurred during our stay away from the Senate. The ploy was successful in the long run in that the bill never was considered. While we were gone, however, the Texas Rangers and other Texas law enforcement agents attempted to locate all of us. In my neighborhood, I had a neighbor who deemed himself as our local patrolman. My neighbor began to notice a suspicious van parked near my home, and one evening quietly snuck up behind the van and confronted the occupants by gunpoint, demanding to know who they were and what they were doing hanging out in our neighborhood. The men showed stark terror and quickly explained that they were members of the Department of Public Safety simply seeking to catch me visiting home so that they could return me to the Senate.

Another amusing incident concerning my absence occurred at the Port Arthur Country Club. I had signed up for a member-guest tournament and since I was to be absent, I asked my son, Carl Jr., to participate in my place. As he stepped forward when my name was called to the beginning T box, two DPS troopers appeared from nearby thinking to arrest me but discovered my teenage son.

The most amusing incident connected with the Killer Bees, however, took place concerning Gene Jones of Houston. After one evening in our secret hiding place in our cramped quarters, Gene vowed if we would consent to let him leave and go to Houston, he would never be captured. He did, in fact, obtain a ride and travelled to Houston. After a day or two, we were called by Senator Jones and that the news would shortly report that he had been captured and was being transported back to Austin so the Senate could re-convene. By this time, the national news media had taken note of the Killer Bee episode and were gathered at the airport where Senator Jones was to be returned in a state guarded helicopter. As the helicopter landed, amid a whole bevy of news media, television cameras, photographers, and reporters accompanied by the sergeant-of-arms of the Senate, the helicopter door opened, and an alleged Senator Jones stepped forward; the sergeant-of-arms stepped forward to take charge. But then sergeant turned to the crowd and said, "This is not Senator Jones!" He quickly asked the identity of the person who had been transported, and he revealed he was Senator Jones' brother. He had been staying at Senator Jones' home and was arrested by Texas Rangers thinking he was the senator as he stepped out to the yard to retrieve the daily newspaper. In good joking fashion, Senator Jones' brother became somewhat famous because T-shirts were quickly printed and worn around the capitol stating, "Set Clayton Jones free."

After finally calculating the time necessary to be gone to defeat consideration of the second primary election bill, we decided to try alleviating some of the criticism on the Department of Public Safety by contacting them to come where we were, pick us up, and deliver us to the capitol, which we did. Our return was quite a news event, but was taken in good humor by most, with some exceptions.

Workers' Comp: Most Frustrating Episode of My Entire Senate Career

The most frustrating episode of my entire Senate career had to do with changing the worker compensation laws of the state. Having been closely associated with labor unions through my father, I entered politics with my primary ambition, as assigned by my father, to stand up for working people. While in the House, I carried the first bill that increased, for the first time in many years, the amount of worker compensation paid to injured workers. I have long held the belief, and still do, that safety in Texas industry has been secondary to making a profit. The low amount paid to injured workers was, to me, an incentive to ignore safety on the grounds that it was cheaper to injure workers than to provide a safe work-place.

One thing that still seems unfair to me is the lack of representation for injured workers in Texas. When a person is charged with a crime under our U.S. Constitution, he cannot be tried without benefit of representation which can be furnished to him, even if poor. Unfortunately, in our worker compensation system, the insurance companies' employers are always represented by very able and skilled counsel. Unfortunately, the same is not true for those injured on the job.

The chambers of commerce and various lobbies for industry in Texas have long put up a howl that we needed to "reform" workers compensation. Basically, their argument was that, if we took lawyers out of the mix, it would expedite payment to workers at a lesser cost. I found the argument of removing lawyers from workers' comp salacious. Even if we would remove lawyers from the worker compensation process, insurance companies and employers would always have their attorney on hand to litigate any issue over injured workers.

As the battle raged, I did my best to oppose so-called reform measures favored by the Texas Association of Business and other well-heeled lobbyists. Unfortunately, any effort to compromise failed. On one occasion, I and several of my like-minded colleagues in the Senate had a bill that would have been accepted by industry, kept lawyers in the mix, and amounted to a nice increase for injured workmen throughout the state. Unfortunately, then president of the Texas Trial Lawyers, David Perry of Corpus Christi, thought he could have a better deal, saying, "I've got sixteen rocks in the Senate," sixteen senators who would vote against my bill. That would allow him to hold out until a deal that suited him was available. Unfortunately, he was dead wrong.

Shortly after this compromise failed, we began to have senators who flaked. Unfortunately, one of them was my good pal, Chet Brooks. I always suspected that he had been unduly influenced by some of his monied supporters out of Houston. Money always seemed to linger about us. A crushing blow came when Lieutenant Governor Hobby caved in and decided it was time to remove the issue from Senate consideration. The industry bill passed, leaving workers in Texas really without representation in contested worker comp matters.

The issue was one that tested my friendship and relations with Lieutenant Governor Hobby. For several months after the bill passed, every story I heard about an abused worker or one unable to find representation in a contested hearing, I would forward it to Governor Hobby with a reminder that it was his doing that allowed it to happen. Fortunately, the friendship between Hobby and me warmed up again, and we remain to this day good friends.

Public and Higher Education

Sooner than expected, I was named as chair of the Senate Education Committee. The committee had jurisdiction of both public education as well as higher education. I knew as soon as Lt.

Governor Hobby appointed me to this position that I faced several challenges in trying to deal with problems throughout the state at both levels.

Public education in Texas was ranked near the bottom nationwide. Public schools have traditionally been underfunded in Texas since the late 50s or early 60s. Some public school districts were so wealthy that they easily produced favorable results for their students while others were less than poor, struggling to provide very meager benefits to their students.

Customarily, Senate bills are directed at amending, adding to, or taking from previous legislation. Generally, after a member of the legislature introduces a particular bill, it becomes like an adopted child. Thereafter, those interested in that particular legislation will seek out the original sponsor in attempts to improve or diminish the effect of such legislation. These adopted children were the reason for numerous bills that I introduced and worked on as a member of the Senate.

One example of ongoing care for legislation has to do with the institutions of learning at Lamar-Port Arthur and Lamar-Orange. When introduced, this legislation provided what we called a "work center" at Port Arthur and Orange, Texas. They operated as a branch or an off-shoot of Lamar University out of Beaumont. Although opposed by many other universities and colleges on the grounds that it would simply detract from their ability to raise funds out of the legislature, we managed to get it passed through both houses of the legislature, primarily with the help of Ben Barnes, who at the time was lieutenant governor. Following legislation while I was in the Senate, however, did help with the establishment of these institutions. For example, a measure to allow each of them to be a free standing, degree granting institution gave both institutions status and greatly improved education opportunities for Southeast Texas.

Later on, when education reform was afoot and we divided the Permanent University Fund among all the branches of A&M and University of Texas, we also created a constitutional fund. Being chairman of the Education Committee at that time, I was able to include both Lamar-Orange and Lamar-Port Arthur in a provision that required a constitutional amount to be set aside for colleges and universities not connected with Texas A&M or the University of Texas. Thus, we secured branches in Port Arthur and Orange a permanent place in the higher education system of the state. Of all legislation that I carried both in the House and the Senate, I am most proud of the creation of the colleges in Port Arthur and Orange. Even though naysayers said that neither school would exceed one or two hundred students, both now are enrolling over 2,000 students a year. Both institutions give opportunities for young and old alike who would not otherwise have an opportunity of higher education. They both have greatly added to the economic and general welfare of the communities where they are located.

Perot Committee

About the time that I was appointed to chair the Senate Education Committee, Mark White was elected governor. White had made large promises to teacher groups that something would be done about the low pay of Texas teachers. The session was drawing near to a close when teacher groups started complaining to White that he had not fulfilled his promise, nor had he given much attention to their plight. In an effort to shore up his position with teachers and public education, White announced that he would create a committee, a super committee no less, to thoroughly investigate public education in Texas. I somewhat suspected that he would name members of the House and Senate to his committee; however, White fooled us all by naming Ross Perot, a Dallas billionaire, to head the committee. As a member of the Senate and as chair of the Education Committee, I was appointed as a member of what became known as the Perot Committee.

Bill Hailey, who at the time was Education Chair in the House, along with a host of educational experts, was appointed to form the Perot Committee. We launched a very thorough investigation of what was wrong with public education in Texas and what were better examples of public education throughout the world. We heard from experts on various European countries, Japan, South America, and others. Perot gave his undivided attention to this committee, using his own paid staff on many occasions and, I am sure, funded much of the efforts of this committee. We met throughout the state and heard from superintendents, teachers, and administrators and faculty in higher education.

The committee traveled so much that I once in jest pointed out to Mr. Perot that he was wearing me out because he had a jet to get all around the country and all I had was a single engine airplane. Perot was extremely concerned about things that detracted from the ability to teach children. One of his examples, which he would repeatedly make in public addresses, was the image of a young man who missed 30 days of his education while showing his prize chicken around the state at various fairs. He also expressed concern at the beginning of our study about extracurricular activities, such as sports, detracting from the ability of students to learn.

One of the most unsolvable problems that we faced and tried to address was the fact that Texas' system for funding public education left some school districts with great wealth and only a minimum of effort of taxing themselves. Other school districts produced meager amounts, even with a great effort of taxing themselves.

We heard from specialists on testing, particularly since Perot was big on testing to see whether students were consistently being successful throughout the state. One idea floated, which I considered to be unproductive, was to develop a test of teacher competency. At the time the only evaluation of teachers was left to the principals, with little or no input from others who might observe the skills involved in teaching. One of the recommendations of the committee was that the state needed a better system with more input from evaluators and not just one person to determine the ability of teachers.

I argued against the so-called competency test because the test was so simple that anyone who could read on a level able to read the *Reader's Digest* could easily pass the test. The test would thus not determine teaching competency and would, in fact, infuriate most teachers. Teachers justifiably saw their Texas state certification at risk by having to take this test.

I recall a delegation led by a female teacher from Houston who confronted me in my office and loudly proclaimed that she thought that we politicians needed to take a competency test. I replied to her that we could not because it was unconstitutional. When she inquired, "How so?" I told her that "if we removed all the ignorance from the legislature, it would no longer be representative government." I quickly discovered that she had no sense of humor. The quote, however, became somewhat noteworthy because Molly Ivins published this quote, and it was picked up broadly throughout the state. As a matter of fact, one book used by my wife in teaching government at Lamar State College-Port Arthur found one chapter that was prefaced by this quote.

The most controversial part of the bill was the "no-pass, no-play." Ag teachers, who were big on livestock shows and the like, and coaches shouted their opposition to the measure. The provision was that any student receiving less than a "C" grade in a particular course at the end of the semester was disqualified from any extra-curricular activities. It passed in the re-write of the education bill and has now been fairly universally accepted as a reasonable restriction on deterring from a quality education while pursuing extra-curricular activities.

The dilemma that was left unsolved and was probably of greater importance than the no-pass-no-play rule and still exists today is finding an efficient way to gain enough funds to deliver an effective, free system of public education to Texas students. The state of Texas tried several provisions, most notably the "Robin Hood Plan." Basically, school taxation and valuations were compared, and when wealthy school districts exceeded a certain amount on the system, they had to relinquish a portion of their taxable income to the state to be redistributed to low wealth school districts.

Funding public education remains an almost unsolvable problem in Texas today. I have always felt that assessing the quality of education should depend on the results. Unfortunately, politicians are generally on an election-year-to-election-year cycle when the evaluation of effective education can only be graded in terms of generations. Another problem in Texas is the disparity of wealth as I have pointed out. I have always believed that competition among school districts should be like sail boat races. Everyone is equipped with the same equipment and operate in the same environment. Then it's easy to determine which is the best crew in the regatta. While we made some improvements in teacher evaluation, it was not perfect by any means. One of my disappointments concerning teacher evaluation is that while the teacher organizations complain of unfair evaluations, none has yet had the courage to submit their own plan which they consider equitable in judging the ability of teachers. After studying the unsolvable problem of public education funding, I am still convinced that an equitable system of funding will never be possible until we cease relying on disparate amounts of property taxes collected. In some districts patrons of the school district are struggling and paying the highest rates allowed by law and producing meager amounts to provide the education of their children. While other districts blessed with natural resources, industries, or other high-dollar assets are able to produce large amounts of money for their school district with a minimum effort on the part of the patrons. In my opinion, this will never be solved unless Texas passes some broad-based tax, such as an income tax, puts all the money in one pot, and divides it evenly among all the school districts. In Texas our system is called the State System of Public

Education when, in fact, it has become a local district system with inadequate state support that has gone from about 70% in the 30s and 40s to about 20% today.

Another section of the education bill created a state school board system. There was a short battle over whether members of the State Board of Education should be elected or appointed by the governor. I probably made a mistake in that I was strongly in favor of an elected board, even though I resisted the urging of Governor Hobby and Ross Perot to accede to their desire to have the board appointed by the governor. Unfortunately, since conservatives have gained the control that they have over politics in Texas, the State Board of Education has given too much attention to the attempt to include religious training and ignored many basic well-proven facts about science in the education curricula. For an example, Texas regulation requires teaching content opposed to the Darwinian system of evolution. Legitimate content is pretty hard to find.

There was, and is to some degree, several arguments over whether or not we should allow prayer in schools. My position is that there is plenty of time and room for prayer at home and that that time and space is seldom used by many of those who are advocates of requiring students to pray at the instruction of a governmental agent, "a teacher." Schools themselves have precious little time as it is.

Even though many of the problems related to education have not been solved in Texas, I am still convinced that great benefits have evolved from the Perot Committee study as well as the legislation passed as a result of the Committee's recommendations.

Part 2 of Perot and Education

After the Supreme Court decision declaring the Texas system of funding education unconstitutional, I pondered greatly on proposed solutions. Unfortunately, we ended up with the Robin Hood System whereby wealthy school districts would have to share excess revenue with poorer school districts. I did have another idea though. At one time in the 40s, the state of Texas funded a greater portion of revenue to support public education. That state portion has gradually gone from 75% to about 30%. To me, it seems logical that we should devise a system where every school district would receive the same amount of money for day-to-day operation. I, therefore, proposed a statewide property tax. The state property tax had been repealed several years previously. It was only a nickel. I calculated that, if all districts were taxed at $1.00 per one-hundred-dollar evaluation, a great deal more money would be raised statewide than the current systems of hit and miss. I proposed the same system to Ann Richards who then was governor, and she thought it made sense to her. Unfortunately, when the press got hold of my idea, they failed to include the part of the bill that would have repealed all other local taxes and replaced it with the $1.00 statewide tax. The bill would have provided that school districts could assess themselves a greater tax, but only for building expansion. Nonetheless, after the press announced my idea, Ann Richards abandoned it, and it fell into disrepute for the rest of the legislative session.

One good thing, however, did come out of the repeal of the state property tax. It was a good deal of money left in the "kitty," and I was able to persuade the other members of the legislature, as I was on the conference committee on appropriations, to allocate a big portion of that to build what is now the Montagne Center for Lamar.

Another phenomenon that I discovered while I was chair of the Senate Education Committee was that teacher groups sometimes were counter productive. While I was chair, the three predominant teacher organizations were Texas State Teachers Association, Classroom Teachers, and the Professional Teachers Organization. While the Classroom teachers and TSTA were very active in endorsing candidates and supporting their agenda, the professional organization refused to participate in politics. Teacher pay and other working conditions of teachers is predominantly dependent on what politics do. Not participating simply removes influence that you might have.

On one occasion, during a hearing on a bill to mandate a non-lunch, free hour for teachers, I was approached by one of the teacher groups asking me to kill one of the identical bills introduced by a competing organization. When asked what the difference between the bills was, he could not tell me other than he wanted his group's name for the publicity.

Another problem with teachers is that no teacher group has ever outlined a system for teacher evaluation. It seems to me that if anyone should know how to evaluate the quality of a teacher, it should be teachers. Yet, they steadfastly refused to participate in this process or suggest a new method on their own.

Another phenomenon when I was chair was the effect of low pay on teachers. I believed then, and I believe now, that teachers should be paid much higher in that we entrust them with the future of our children. To measure this phenomenon, I had my staff do a statewide survey. We polled the top graduates of a variety of schools—rural, urban, small, and large throughout the state. The question to the top scholars was: "Would you consider being a schoolteacher?" Only one out of ten said they would even consider it, and of those few who would consider it, the majority of them were children of teachers.

Being an advocate for higher pay for teachers, I emphasized higher pay as attracting better teachers in a speech I gave at Baylor University. Following the speech, I was approached by a young ministerial student who told me that I was wrong to emphasize pay because teaching like preaching was a calling from God. I responded to him by telling him that I had been a Baptist all my life, but I had never observed a Baptist preacher being called by God to a lower paying church.

In addition to the challenges related to public education as I assumed the chairmanship of education in the Senate, there were other challenges related to higher education. Since my tenure as chair of education in the Senate, the job has been bi-furcated in that there is a chairman for higher education and a chairman for public education.

As I assumed leadership in the education field, there were many problems related to unfair distribution of resources related to our colleges and universities. Unfortunately, for many years many colleges who primarily catered to minority groups were not treated fairly on the same basis as what we have now labeled our "flagship institutions." Some of those colleges were Prairie View, Texas Southern, Pan American (now University of Texas Rio Grande Valley), and several others. A glaring example was the fate of Prairie View and others in that the Permanent University Fund established to assist the University of Texas and Texas A&M were sparingly beneficial to other colleges and universities. Prairie View A&M for example, was in fact, a part of Texas A&M as it was created, yet it received little, or no, substantial support from the Permanent University Fund.

One of the major areas of legislation that I am proud to have worked on was upgrading many colleges which resulted in the forced sharing of the Permanent University Fund and the creation of another constitutional funding arrangement to benefit all colleges not falling under the umbrella of UT or A&M. Pan American University, for example, was placed under the umbrella of the University of Texas while Texas A&I became Texas A&M in Kingsville. Prairie View began to receive a greater share of the Permanent University Fund as did those branches or those under the umbrella of the University of Texas. The second constitutional fund set aside a certain amount of annual funds raised for colleges like Lamar University, Sam Houston, or Stephen F. Austin. These reforms in higher education have made colleges and universities available to more Texans and has been greatly beneficial to the future of Texas as a whole.

While I was critical of the Coordinating Board in my early political career, I came to better understand and appreciate its value. Ironically, I had so opposed the gentleman who headed the Coordinating Board as I left the House and joined the Senate that I once decreed, as I became chair of the Education Committee, that his days were numbered. Strangely enough, I came to know him better as we developed a mutual appreciation for one another. We were able to better coordinate between colleges, junior colleges, and various universities throughout the state. We were able to aid the transference of courses and to develop and weed out courses not truly dedicated to higher education or improving the lot of Texas college graduates.

My effort to enforce my long-held belief that pedagogy alone was not the answer to improving public education was seriously controversial, particularly among educators. It was, and still is, my belief for example that a math teacher should concentrate his or her studies on mathematics, not on a formula on how to teach mathematics. It was my belief at the time, which I later decided was well founded, that there were too many "busy work" type courses taught in order to acquire a degree and sometimes a graduate degree in the field of education. I proposed successfully to abolish a simple education degree and replace it with requirements that teachers complete a course of study in the field they seek to teach. During the debate, I was successful in persuading my fellow members of the legislature that I was right by simply showing a catalog which listed the requirements for a graduate degree in education at the University of Texas. For example, the catalog listed a course with credits toward a graduate degree in the effective use of the felt board. A felt board was simply a device to entertain preschool and grade school students as they entered public education. The change has been an improvement in the field of teaching throughout our state, and computers have replaced the poor felt board.

Unfortunately, Texas has not solved the problem of an uneven funding of public education and the lack of adequate funding for our colleges and universities. It was shocking to me to learn that less than 25% of funds going to the University of Texas and Texas A&M were public funds. Unfortunately, more and more outside funds from private contributions, corporate endowments, foundation funding and other sources fund our public colleges and universities, particularly our flagship institutions. This trend continues to grow today and is the next big challenge for colleges and universities nationwide.

Bullock

I served with two very strong lieutenant governors. Bill Hobby was satisfied to let matters play out on the floor of the Senate. He would receive input no matter how diverse, and then he would work with what he got. Bullock was a master at forcing compromise. He skirted the open government rules by discussing many issues in his office during what he called "committee chair meetings."

Bullock seemed to be totally reluctant to allow meaningful debate on the floor of the Senate. Fortunately for me, before Bullock became lieutenant governor, I kind of established myself with him. While Bullock was comptroller of the state, an issue arose concerning whether or not the state would allow members of public employees' unions to have automatic dues checkoff. In other words, employees' paychecks automatically would have union dues deducted and sent to the union of their choice. Bullock, swimming upstream in a conservative state, authorized dues checkoff for employees of the comptroller's office.

Shortly after this action, I ran into Bullock one evening at one of his favorite local watering holes and dining facilities. As usual, he was well into his "cups." This was the time before he took the "dry-out" lessons which reformed him as an alcoholic. Bullock was always a bully and was unrestrained in assaulting an opinion of any with whom he disagreed. He approached me, I suppose, because he thought I was a spokesman for labor. Basically, he started ranting about the fact that labor was unappreciative of his risky maneuver in allowing the checkoffs. He went on as though somehow I was responsible for the lack of appreciation of his bravery. As he began to address me with cursing and threats, I looked him in the eye and told him, "Bullock, you are much smaller than I am, and if you think I will abide you getting in my face, cursing me, or insulting me, you better change your attitude because I am not above knocking the crap out of you in a public place." He quietly backed down and that was the end of the conversation.

Unfortunately for Bullock, that particular evening he was admitted to the hospital with a serious heart attack. The following morning, however, his number one aid appeared in my office to tell me that Bullock had directed him to find me and profusely apologize for his conduct toward me the evening before. Not wanting to miss an opportunity to goad him a little more, I told the aid that I wished he would tell Bullock that I knew for a fact that he had not had a heart attack, that he had faked it in order to avoid facing me with an apology in person. That seemed to gain me a new respect from Bullock, which followed me throughout his term as lieutenant governor. We became fast friends, and I became one of his lead senators when it came to his pet legislation. The same was true when he selected me and asked that I carry the legislation to combine five of the environmental type agencies into one, which gave birth to the Texas CEQ.

Of all the politicians I have had the experience of working with and against, Bullock possessed the greatest political sense. He was unparalleled in gauging which way the political winds were blowing. As an example, Bullock for a short period of time advocated an income tax for Texas. If well studied and real math is applied, the average homeowner in Texas would fare better taxwise by an income tax patterned after the states which have one, rather than the ever-escalating taxes on homesteads and business properties. Only a short time after Bullock responded to the wide-spread opposition to the idea of an income tax, he then advocated placing a ban on income tax in our state's constitution which was indeed offered, passed, and is a part of our constitution now.

Bullock was a reformed alcoholic, and in some sense, he was like an evangelist for drying out. Not only did he want to refrain from drinking, he decided he wanted everyone else to do so likewise.

Both Bullock and Ann Richards, to their credit, had attended a "dry-out" clinic in California. Bullock previously, as lieutenant governor, would host all the committee chairs in his office for a round of drinks, usually lasting too long. On his return from the clinic, however, the drinking bouts turned into lectures about how we should refrain from the use of alcohol.

Bullock could be charming at times, but many times completely overbearing and so blunt as to be downright rude. On one occasion one of my friends, a most generous supporter and well-heeled lawyer, met with Bullock in a meeting I arranged to offer him a $100,000 contribution. As they were discussing matters, my friend explained to Bullock that he was about to give him $100,000 but that Bullock would have to listen to him and do as he bid. Bullock immediately rose, told the would-be donor that he could take his contribution and stick it you know where, and strolled out of the room without further ado.

Smarter Than I

My success in the Senate was due mainly to the fact that I was able to hire the assistants who were often smarter than I. It is a blessing to have a good number one assistant helping to run your office. Before I left the House, I was able to employ Dora McDonald, a very smart former school teacher who fit into a political job like she had trained for it. Dora stayed with me until the governor appointed her to a statewide office controlling the creation of new hospitals.

Before Dora left for bigger things, I hired Caryn Cosper who had been assistant to Congressman Patman when he was in the U.S. Congress. I commented to Caryn that she appeared to be over qualified. Her response was that she was tired of being the top in the office and would like to have a job that would not require so much thought and simply pecking on a typewriter. I was fortunate to be able to hire Caryn who later became my number one aid until my term in the Senate finished.

When I became chair of the Senate Education Committee, I inherited some extremely capable help in the form of Sally Haenelt as well as Terry Heller, who had a Ph.D. in education. As a bonus, she was a great musician who could play both by music and ear. Terry furnished many hours of pleasant diversion from the humdrum day-in, day-out of duties attached to political office.

As I became chair of Economic Development, my long-time young friend, James Fields, whom I had known since he was in kindergarten with my oldest daughter, became my number one assistant and helped run that committee. James went on after I left the Senate to become one of the leaders of the Texas Trial Lawyers Association where he remains today.

Of course, local assistants were critical to maintain a position in the Senate. I was blessed with a great secretary who could probably easily have passed the bar exam, Elizabeth "Tissie" Stansbury, who stayed with me over 30 years until we both retired from the active practice of law.

Marty Craig was not only a good assistant doing casework in my local Senate office but also was very helpful politically in that she had been a realtor and very active in civic affairs both in Orange and Jefferson Counties. Marty seemed to know everybody and never met a stranger. She was very pleasant and brought humor and good work to the local Senate office which was in Beaumont, Texas.

I feel a certain amount of pride in the fact that the great majority of people employed through my Senate office have been very successful in later careers. Marty Craig, for example, went on to work for other state agencies. Caryn Cosper did the same. James Fields is now the titular head of the Texas Trial Lawyers Association. Sally Haenelt-Cain obtained a very important federal position related to education. And Dr. Terry Heller is now a member of the city council where she resides in Wiscasset. Two young men who in effect were employed in the office as "gofers" and assistants have shown great promise in their adulthood. Frankie Martin is now the administrator of a large real estate holding, and David Gonzalez is working as a lobbyist on a nationwide basis in the field of insurance. I am sure their success is more based on their talents than my tutelage.

Although not a member of my staff, Carlton Turner, who was Seargent of Arms of the Senate most of the time while I was a member, was most helpful in many ways. On one occasion I recall a photographer taking photographs of action in the Senate demanding that a member of the Senate step aside and stop obstructing his view. The senator involved at the time responded the expletive F...., he said, "I am a member of the Senate." Carlton took charge of the situation and banished the photographer to the Senate gallery and revoked his privileges to be on the Senate floor. An outgrowth of this incident fell on me in that the incident was videoed by a Houston television station which made it appear when relating the news item about the occurrence that I had been the senator uttering the obscenity. This occurred because at the time I was speaking to the Senate, and although it had nothing to do with the reported incident, it appeared on national news that I was the guilty senator. I had Turner vouch for the fact that I was not the guilty participant which did not deter Sam Donaldson on ABC from reporting it as though I had been. I sent a letter Donaldson in care of ABC demanding a retraction and a correction of the nationally reported incident. I received a form letter back from the attorney for ABC saying that they stood on the accuracy of their reporting and would have no further comment on the subject. When I threatened to file suit, I received no answer whatsoever. I then filed another letter with ABC and a copy to Donaldson. I told him that if I did not hear some response to my complaint within a certain period of time it was my intent to file suit for $9.00 in damages in the justice court of Bridge City, Texas. A skilled attorney would realize that a $9.00 judgement in justice court could only be appealed directly to the Supreme Court of the United States. I further reminded Donaldson that there was little airline service to and from Bridge City, Texas. With this threat, I did receive a response and eventually a letter which by agreement allowed me to publish it correcting the misstatement on the national news. As a post script to this incident, not long afterward, I happened to encounter Donaldson in the Senatorial offices of the outlying state office building. I introduced myself. He chuckled and remembered that I had been the senator who had threatened to take him to justice court.

Celebrations

Celebrations throughout my tenure as senator were highlights and enjoyable events of my career in politics. One of my political events that probably helped me stay in office as much as any was my Labor Day Picnic. The picnic became an event statewide for democratic officeholders and candidates who were seeking office on a statewide basis. A Labor Day picnic was held at the Beaumont Fair Grounds with organized labor handling and serving the food. The faculty from Lamar oversaw various games from volleyball to a dunking booth, and at least three bands appeared at the function. At the last Labor Day Picnic, Senator Lloyd Bentsen, candidate for vice-president, appeared. We served 10,000 plates of barbecue. One of my friends had acquired a nice white horse and buggy. He wanted to show it off by having Senator Bentsen ride in the buggy and make a round in the rodeo arena. Unfortunately, during the ride around the arena, the horse became spooked by all the clapping and yelling by the crowd. The horse took the bit in his teeth and started to trot much faster than my friend had anticipated. As they passed the bandstand, you could see the terrified looks on the faces of Senator Bentsen and my friend who was driving.

Another fun event in my career was "Governor for a Day." It is customary during a session and sometimes afterward for the governor of Texas along with the lieutenant governor to absent themselves from the state of Texas. On such an occasion, the president pro-tempore is elevated to be governor. The same would occur due to the death or resignation of the governor and lieutenant governor. The absence of the governor and lieutenant governor is usually planned and a celebration is planned for the president pro-tempore. This occurred for me and was a great celebration because it followed my acquittal and clearing from the false indictments that had been returned against me. The Lamar University choir sang from the balcony of the Senate chamber. My wife and I entered the chamber under the raised swords of the Ross Volunteers of A&M and Dr. Hans Marc, president of the University of Texas, spoke. My aunt, Addie Mae Williams, a Pentecostal minister, and my African American friend, Ransom Howard of the First Sixth Street Baptist Church in Port Arthur, Texas, led the assembled group in prayer. My friends from Chambers County in the seafood business prepared a great fish fry on the grounds of the capitol. As a side note, the morning following my day as governor, I hosted a breakfast to thank those who had weighed in and helped provide such a wonderful event. As I reached the hotel where I was hosting the breakfast, a large banner strung over the room and bumper stickers were placed strategically around the room saying, "Gee, I Miss Governor Parker."

Unfortunately, holding public office involves trying to stay elected. To that end, it is essential in today's political arena to have adequate funds to carry your message to the would-be voters. As a result, even birthdays turn out to be celebrations geared to help raise funds to be used in the coming election. To this end, I was aided by a very able college professor. Dr. Charles Turco was a professor of biology at Lamar University but extremely skilled in putting together fundraisers. Over the many years I occupied the Senate seat, we were successful in raising many thousands of dollars at birthday celebrations with different themes.

It was helpful to my own career that I had earned my spurs in organization. A good example of one was I sponsored a union fundraiser early in my career in support of then U.S. Senator Ralph Yarbrough. We were able to put together a celebration at the Oil Chemical and Atomic Workers' union hall in Port Arthur. As an attraction we were favored with a one-man concert by Willie Nelson. At the time, Willie had not gained the notoriety he now enjoys, and although we had a nice crowd, it was far from one that filled the large union hall.

If anyone desires to remain in elective office more than one term, fundraising is an essential function to the practice of politics. Fortunately for me, I had the able assistance of Dr. Charles Turco. Although not my official finance chairman, Turco was a whiz at organizing fundraising events such as birthdays, celebrations of political victories, and recognition of legislative accomplishments.

No doubt, I owe Turco a great deal of appreciation for the yeoman's job he did in this capacity.

Unfortunately, in the election of 1994, I ran for re-election and was opposed by Michael Galloway from Montgomery County. Galloway had no experience in government. Although he claimed to be in the oil and gas business, his involvement was generally up-keep, mowing, and cleanup of well sites. My district had been changed during the past regular session to include more of Harris County and changed even further by order of the court due to a Republican lawsuit. I was given the high-dollar areas of Kingwood along with more of Harris County. My political consultant assured me that his polls showed me well ahead by 10-14 points, but unfortunately for my political career, Jefferson County had the lowest voter turnout in recent years. I, along with long-time friend and congressman, Jack Brooks, was defeated. As a postscript, however, Mr. Galloway to my knowledge passed no significant legislation and was deemed by the *Texas Monthly Magazine* as one of the worst members of the Texas Senate.

Looking back, I can see that in 1994 the state and my district had grown away from me. It has grown farther away since I left. That label that I first got when I entered politics still held true to the public at large. I was still a "unionist liberal." The funny thing about labels is that they are attached to you by others; you don't create them or earn them. A second funny thing about this label is that by 1994 there were very few of us "unionist liberals" in the Texas legislature or my district, so very few of us got elected or can get elected, yet those running for office tend to blame a lot on the "unionist liberals" who can't get elected and have little or no power.

I saw a lot of political changes, but the most recent one left me behind. By 1994, social media was just starting to show up, and we had around the clock news. As was starting then, the state or national audience split and kept splitting some more right up until today. In this era, citizens had their own media platforms; what voters wanted was what they wanted, not what would work, what was needed, or what was wrong. Voters (or even non-voters) could have their own heroes and villains and then band with other voters (or even non-voters) to vote (or not vote) for their heroes or against their villains—or not vote but raise a lot of social media ruckus. And there I was and here I am peddling facts and figures and procedure and law and politics.

In my career in the Senate, I was the lead sponsor for almost 200 bills. Many were mundane matters ordinarily required of a state senator. Many of these matters, for example, included authorizing drainage districts, sewer districts, authorization of local bond issues, and countless other mundane things needed in various parts of one senatorial district. There were also countless congratulatory and other type resolutions commending good citizenship and various kinds of accomplishments, even for high school graduates.

I am proud, however, of being the sponsor of several major pieces of legislation that remain on the books, many of which have had a positive impact on the quality of life in our state. Most of these involved an adventure into the rules, habits, and inner workings of not only the Senate, but the House and relationships with the governor of Texas. These pieces of legislation regarded worker compensation, education (both public and higher), environmental matters and related agencies, water safety, and support and protection of schools in my senatorial district.

There were more minor skirmishes relating to resolutions to Congress, hunting in state parks, degree-granting for Lamar State College at Orange and Port Arthur, and the creation of new programs at Lamar University in Beaumont including the creation of the Academy of Leadership in the Humanities and The Dishman School of Nursing. Unfortunately, some measures were not lasting, even though they were popular, and they could have worked had they been continued.

Doing good work and passing bills make up only half of the formula necessary to be a leader in the Texas legislature. First, you have to be elected. Probably the guidance from my father, who was a political animal as a labor leader, saw me through my years in the House, but the Senate was a whole new ballgame. Fortunately for me, I had a group of core supporters spread out throughout the senatorial district that held me in good stead for the eighteen and a half years I was able to represent the people of the fourth senatorial district.

Bill Dickson, a Beaumont architect and aviator, became one of my closest advisers and friends; often flying me back and forth from Jefferson County to Austin in his plane. Bill was quite a fellow, but oftentimes had me on edge doing his flying. Bill had a habit before each takeoff to pray for a safe trip in a loud voice in a closed-up airplane. I always thought it was somewhat amusing, but at the same time a little scary that my pilot on an air trip was seeking to pray before a takeoff.

The core of my Beaumont support lies in the Board of Regents for Lamar University, led by Dr. John Gray. Dr. Gray had been head of Lamar Tech before it became Lamar University. He was president of one of the largest banks in Beaumont. Otho Plummer was on the board and was a former city councilman. Tom Maes, also on the board, ended up being my finance chairman.

Of course, labor was always in my core of support, led by Harry Hubbard, president of the state AFL-CIO, Frank Arnaud, president of the Sabine Area Labor Council, Andy Jackson and a host of labor guys who were always there to put up signs, do mail-outs, call, and otherwise give me tremendous support at election time.

Bob Montagne was a purchasing agent for the hospital in Orange County and became my go-to guy in Orange County along with H.D. Pate, city attorney with Bridge City. I was able to reward Bob Montagne toward the end of my career by influencing the state and Lamar University to name the fine gymnasium and athletic center as the Montagne Center. Although Bob Montagne never had the benefit of a college education, he was one of the wisest men ever to assist me in my political career. He probably appreciated a college education more than the average person because he was never able financially to obtain one. Fortunately, Montagne's children did so in grand manner.

The Black community always supported me overwhelmingly, led in part by Rev. Ransom Howard, pastor of one of the larger churches in Port Arthur and LeRoy Bell, a community activist with whom I had worked as a laborer during summers at Gulf Refinery. Elmo Willard, an attorney from Beaumont, was also one of my fiercest supporters, urging people to not only support me but to oppose anyone critical of me in the community.

Jimmy Berkman was my man in Liberty County, a banker, oil man, and influential in banking and business throughout Liberty. Cindy Jenkins and the Jackson family were my go-to people in Chambers County, carrying it every election in which I was a candidate.

So, while I was in the Texas legislature, I was, as the old joke from Mark Twain or Alex Haley or Bill Clinton said, like a turtle on a post. When you see a turtle on a post, you know that he didn't get there on his own.

Part IV: The Indictment

Unhappy Times at Happy Times

The story of my involvement with the Jefferson County law enforcement and grand jury system must begin with my introduction of Danny Lee. Danny Lee was a hail-fellow-well-met man and a great athlete, having lettered in three sports at Colorado State. When I met Danny Lee later in life, he was a great golfer holding the course record at the Pleasure Island Port Arthur golf course. I believe it was in the low 60s that he scored.

Danny became a client early upon my return from the Navy to open my law office in Port Arthur. Danny was in the business of providing coin-operated machines to various establishments—bars, cafes, and the like. Danny became a great client, not only sending me his business, but also other matters that he ran across in the many facilities where he operated.

Danny not only became a client but a good friend. He presented me early on with a new set of golf clubs and vowed to teach me to become an average or better golfer. He failed in this endeavor. Danny, however, continued to be a great golfer, probably making part of his living on the golf course. He apparently had a regular, weekly game with many businessmen and golfers at the Port Arthur Country Club for which he informed me that he had netted about four to five hundred dollars a week.

The whole story of Happy Times Video began in my office located on Stadium Road. A member of my Lion's Club came in one day and explained that he had purchased a home on the GI Bill but in the meantime had recently had to be the tennis pro at the country club in Lafayette, Louisiana, an offer that he did not want to refuse. He explained that his problem was that he had signed only a month or two before to purchase a house, using his GI Bill benefits. Because I had recently had dealings with this program, I told him that it was a simple matter to exit the obligation created by his GI Bill financing. All that was necessary was to find someone with decent credit, or credit equal to his, to take over the loan and assume ownership of the house. After learning that his equity was only about six or seven hundred dollars, which he agreed to forgo, I then agreed that I would assume the indebtedness and take over ownership of the house. At the time, Danny Lee happened to be in the office and overheard the conversation. Danny told me that, if I allowed him half interest in the deal, he would see that the house was rented and the note paid each month. Sounding like a wonderful deal by which I would obtain ownership in a house without paying any money, I agreed to the deal with Danny. The house was in Griffin Park, Texas, a part of Port Arthur.

After only a few months, Danny was unable to locate a suitable tenant for the house so decided to occupy it himself and pay the note which was fairly low—probably less than three hundred dollars a month.

Things went well for several years with Danny running his business, but then he got himself in a jam by failing to pay his income tax for many years. Danny also began having trouble making even the small payment on the house note.

Since Danny was living in the house alone, having divorced, and was unable to make the monthly payments, I began looking for ways to pay the note on the house. Examining the house, I figured that it could easily be divided, so I set about having improvements made by creating a front apartment using the front bedroom and living room. I placed a bathroom facility in this room and closed one of the doors leading to the other part of the house. I was concerned about someone occupying the apartment, however, and being unable to escape in the event of fire or some other mishap. I therefore created a storage closet at the beginning of the hallway leading to the other part of the house. We put a door with a flimsy latch on it to close off the backside of the closet but created an escape hatch for emergencies in the apartment. The apartment project went well for several months. Danny, having good connections, would frequently rent the apartment on a short-term basis to seamen and various other workmen whom he knew to be in town temporarily.

The real trouble began when Danny, to make a few bucks and being very clever, figured out a way to break the code on tape cartridges. He began to rent or buy pornographic tapes from nearby shops in Port Arthur and copy them. Eventually, Danny had five or ten video machines busy copying his pornographic material. When he proudly showed the operation to me, I suggested to him that it was not a good idea and that he could get in trouble. He responded by pointing out that there were at least three shops in Port Arthur openly selling the same material from which he was renting them or purchasing them. At the time, I didn't have any concern over violation of copyright laws. Danny was selling several under the label of "Happy Times Video" and undercutting the regular retail stores by about thirty bucks a pop. I told him that I did not see any legal problem with the sales.

Danny being a friend of several years, I would occasionally stop by to check on him since his health was not good and he appeared to be somewhat lonesome in view of the fact that not only had he been abandoned by his wife but by several of his girlfriends. Danny, to further buttress his argument that he was not doing anything illegal, pointed out to me that several of his tapes had been borrowed on more than one occasion by the Port Arthur Police Department for their annual Christmas stag event.

Danny Doyle and the DA

Danny Doyle and I became partners at the law office. Danny had been a longtime assistant district attorney, and I thought he would bring a new dimension to my law practice which was primarily labor, personal injuries, and business law with a smattering of criminal law. The partnership worked well for a while in that Danny attracted many criminal clients and added to the gross income of the Parker-Doyle Law Firm.

Danny Doyle had little regard for the then district attorney, Jim McGrath, whom Danny believed to be not only a poor lawyer, but also one of doubtful ethical credentials. Ironically, in all probability, my dad, Harvie Parker, being very persuasive, was key to McGrath having been appointed to the position he occupied.

Then, two events occurred which put both Danny and me at odds with Mr. McGrath. First, a young man, a minor represented by my new partner, Danny Doyle, had been called into McGrath's office without notification to Danny as his lawyer. He was persuaded without benefit of counsel to plead guilty to a charge that we believe he could have been acquitted of if tried. Contact with a lawyer's client without notice to his lawyer is a serious offense under the state bar cannons of ethics. Danny was so enraged that McGrath had done this and victimized this young client that he filed a formal grievance with the state bar against McGrath. The grievance was upheld, and McGrath, to his embarrassment, received a public reprimand, which was published in the state bar journal. As one might imagine, relations between Danny Doyle and Jim McGrath were, to say the least, very frigid.

Another event that further put our little firm at odds with Mr. McGrath involved a runaway grand jury that was supposedly investigating our Port Arthur Independent School District. The chairman of the grand jury, Larry Steflen, was a self-described labor leader who had been an officer in the OCAW Local 23. Larry and others decided to restructure the hierarchy of the management of the PAISD via the grand jury process. This grand jury ultimately indicted the superintendent as well as the assistant superintendent. I was employed to represent the assistant superintendent whose name was Fleener.

Mr. Fleener had taken a trip to an educational conclave; he was entitled to do so at district expense. Fleener had explained to me that he and several officials had pooled their money and rather than rent individual rooms, had rented a fairly nice suite of rooms together. Apparently, Mr. Fleener either cheated somewhat on his expense account or kept really poor records concerning his claim for expenses. The records appeared as though he had substantially overcharged the district for the trip. I accompanied Mr. Fleener when he was subpoenaed to appear before the grand jury. He, in fact, testified. Following his interview, we were approached by Larry Steflen as well as Mr. McGrath, the then district attorney. The two of them informed us that, unless Mr. Fleener resigned immediately, McGrath and Steflen would return to the grand jury and have him indicted on that day. Since Fleener figured out that his future opportunities with the PAISD were limited, he was more than willing to resign; but as his attorney and at his urging, I requested of McGrath and Steflen that he at least be given to the end of the school year to resign so that he could seek other employment of a similar kind. McGrath and Steflen were unrelenting in their demands, and since Fleener did not resign that day, he was indicted.

The trouble with this little scenario is that a demand made of someone to perform certain acts under threat of being indicted if they refuse is a crime like bribery. In Fleener's case, we were able to have his charges reduced to a misdemeanor to which he pled, paid a fine, and escaped any jail time. Unfortunately, however, Fleener's career as a school administrator suffered serious damage, making it difficult, well near impossible, for him to find other comparable employment.

Fleener employed Larry Watts, a Houston attorney who specializes in civil rights litigation, to represent him in a suit against the school district and all members of the grand jury including the district attorney. I was subpoenaed by Watts in the Fleener trial which took place in the U.S. District Court of the Eastern District of Texas. In a conversation with Watts, McGrath told Watts, that were I to testify, he would see that I would sorely regret choosing sides and testifying against him in the trial. The trial resulted in an approximately $400,000 judgment in favor of Fleener against members of the grand jury as well as Mr. McGrath. This occurrence also did not help the Parker and Doyle firm's relationship with the Jefferson County District Attorney's office.

The Indictment

It was a year when I was in session in the Senate, but I would usually come home on Thursdays so I could practice some law on Friday, Saturday, and Sunday. I was at the courthouse when someone told me there had been a big raid in the city of Port Arthur. On checking what had been raided, I discovered the house in Griffin Park where Danny Lee lived had been the subject of a high-profile police operation. The van used to check fingerprints was there. Four cop cars had surrounded the place. And the police had done a search of Danny Lee's home, including the entire building owned by Danny and me. The television billed the raid as one stemming from pornography, which I found a little strange. I found it strange since the Police Association of Port Arthur had borrowed Danny's dirty movies on at least two occasions for their Christmas stag party. I contacted McGrath while I was at the courthouse and informed him that I was part owner of the house but had nothing to do with Danny's operation of making dirty movies. He made some comment, seeming to make light of the whole affair.

I later reviewed all the newspaper articles as well as the TV coverage and could see that more was made of it than should have been. I went back to Austin the following Monday and began to hear rumors that I was being looked at by the grand jury. I had little concern because I knew that I had nothing to do with Danny's operation and had some doubts as to whether Danny's operation was illegal in the first place. I did have some concern over the grand jury; it appeared that almost a majority of the twelve-person grand jury had been on the school board that I had testified against and that Mr. Fleener had gotten a judgment against. Not only were there many former school board members on the grand jury, but some who had a close connection to those on the school board. As an example, a neighbor of one of the members of the school board against whom the judgment was rendered was on the grand jury. I went about my business but kept hearing that they were looking at clients of mine, trying to find some way to involve me in the grand jury investigation concerning the house in Griffin Park. I further learned that the grand jury was not being presided over by an attorney, but by Calise Blanchard, an ex-Port Arthur cop.

131

I was invited to appear before the grand jury. Unfortunately, I made the same mistake many of my clients have made in the past. I was hesitant to carry in an attorney because I was afraid it would appear that I had something to fear and needed to have a lawyer. In the grand jury, I was asked whether or not I had met with a reputed drug dealer named Tweedle on February 17. After checking my pocket calendar, I was certain I had not; I was in Austin attending a session of the legislature on that date. Later, this would prove to be very significant. The question was based on a tape recording the grand jury had listened to in which I was accused of having a discussion with Mr. Tweedle. The tape recording was made by Richard Bennett, husband of Rene' Bennett, former partner of Fern Roos. I had formed Fernee's Catering company as their lawyer without charge. I had, in fact, represented Richard in a couple of matters. Richard was given to peddling marijuana and bookmaking in downtown Port Arthur. I later learned that the recorded conversation between Tweedle and me took place in the lobby of my office upon a chance meeting when Tweedle informed me that he was very likely to need my services soon. My simple reply was, "Call me." I never heard back from Tweedle, nor did I hear anything about Tweedle until the grand jury returned the indictment claiming that I lied about meeting with Tweedle at Danny Lee's house.

In about two weeks, again when I was back in Port Arthur for the weekend from the legislative session, I got a call from McGrath to inform me the grand jury had handed down not one indictment but two against me: one for production of salacious material and one for solicitation of prostitution. The word spread rather quickly; I was devastated of course, but one consoling factor was that my distant cousin, Oscar Wyatt, a multi-millionaire whom I had represented over 50 years, flew his helicopter to Port Arthur and landed near my office. He came in where we were ensconced in my office to let me know he was fully behind me and would support me any way he could. Wyatt said in his inimitable fashion, "What if I just called the son-of-a-bitch and tell him that I've got a million dollars that I will spend all of to make his life miserable if he doesn't drop this thing?" I urged Wyatt not to make such a threat because I didn't believe it would help but only make matters worse. Wyatt then asked me what it was that I thought I would need. I told him that obviously I would need quite a bit of money for a defense team. Wyatt immediately picked up the phone in my office, called his office, reached his secretary, Jo. "Jo," he said, "I want you to put $200,000 in Carl's account so that these bastards will understand he will not hurt for money." I received many calls of encouragement from those who believed I was innocent and was assured by many that I would be supported in the community.

The press, of course, had a field day. The local senator had been indicted. I called for a press conference, which I held after hiring Tom Hanna, the former district attorney, as my lead counsel. We gathered in the large conference room of Hanna's law firm. I was surrounded by probably 20-30 representatives of newspapers and radio and television stations throughout the community. I explained to them that I was innocent, that I thought it was a clique of badly motivated police officers who had designed to bring me down politically. I also asked that they bear with me in that I intended to continue my duties as senator and that I would not be commenting on the charges. It would be difficult to do so and at the same time maintain a defense.

One local character, Jack Pieper, who was a local disc jockey with whom I had had kind of a fun relationship, had a habit when interviewing of sticking his entire tape recorder in your face, not just a microphone. So true to form, he knelt beside my chair at the head of the big conference table and stuck the recorder in my face and said, "Carl, I take it that you maintain that you are innocent of these charges." I looked at him and said, "Jack, you know very well the only dirty movies I have ever seen are the ones with you and the young boys." Of course, it was a joke; the whole crew of reporters and press people knew it was a joke, but Piper fell on his butt and dropped his tape recorder. Later on, he saw the humor. This ended the press conference, I thought, on a good note. And most of the press honored the commitment not to question me about the indictment when interviewing me about political matters connected with serving in the Senate.

The mainstream press, including the Austin press, did give me some help. After checking my attendance in the Senate, reporters found that, on the day the grand jury claimed I had met with a drug dealer in Port Arthur, I was, in fact, making a speech on the floor of the Senate. The district attorney's response to this revelation was to quickly go to a second grand jury and attempt to re-indict me using a different date. The effort failed and the whole episode of the wrong date began to cast serious doubt on the validity of the charge.

Molly Ivins, a well-known political writer, not only in Texas but nation-wide, wrote a rather humorous article showing the ridiculous claim that I had made enough money with a two-prostitute operation to construct my new home, which was under construction at the time. All this helped, at least in the public's perception, and I ended up being re-elected without opposition.

The Prisoner and Calise Blanchard

After the indictment was well underway, my attorney, John Hanna, received a call from a person who said he was in jail at the old sub-courthouse jail in Port Arthur, Texas. This was a facility which was seldom used since the 60s and a call from there was somewhat unusual. The person told Hanna that he was being held there by Calise Blanchard, the assistant district attorney (not a lawyer), and had been transferred there from the Texas prison system. He further told Hanna that he was being abused and being forced to give statements about me that were not true. Hanna contacted someone in authority through normal channels; that person denied that the prisoner even existed, let alone was being held in the Port Arthur sub-courthouse jail.

Hanna then contacted Wayne Reaud and suggested that Reaud represent this person and attempt to locate him. Reaud was somewhat reluctant to do so saying that he was not into criminal defense and did not really know the proper procedures. Because he was my friend, however, Reaud finally agreed and managed to contact someone affirming the man was being held. Reaud and Hanna called on Judge King, a district judge, to hold a hearing which King agreed to on a Saturday morning while the courthouse was closed. After reaching the hearing, King instructed the sheriff's department to produce the man under penalty of contempt if they did not.

The man claimed he had contacted the district attorney's office indicating he might have some information about me. After being promised favors, perhaps even cutting the length of his sentence, he was transferred to Jefferson County and placed in the Port Arthur jail. He demanded certain privileges, including special treatment and access to a phone. Fortunately for me, Blanchard left the man too long, and he became upset and told Blanchard that he had made the story up and would not testify, nor would he sign a document prepared by Blanchard incriminating me in any criminal activities. The man claimed that Blanchard beat him and threatened to kill him if he did not follow through with his promise to testify to things which were untrue. The man revealed all of this in the hearing before Judge King, who was extremely unhappy and ordered him back to prison.

This incident created yet another episode in the ability of Calise Blanchard, the sheriff, and district attorney, to frame me for some crime.

Preparation for the Fight

Armed with Wyatt's $200,000 loan, I set about preparing to defend myself. Upon Wyatt's recommendation, I hired a tough little investigator, a former member of Coastal Corporation security team, to help me investigate everything concerning the charges against me. In addition to Tom Hanna, former district attorney of Jefferson County, I hired John Hannah, a former U.S. attorney for the Eastern District of Texas and an old friend of mine from the legis- lature. Also, I hired Walter Seakaly, best described as a "jailhouse lawyer," with a great deal of experience in defending criminal cases in Jefferson County and a former close associate and friend of Jim McGrath, for whom Seakaly had very little respect. On one occasion with my three lawyers, Beverly and I were sitting around the pool discussing strategies. Seakaly opined that I was the second innocent person he had had the privilege of representing.

With the help of my lawyers' connections and my private investigator, Keith Budd, we were discovering numerous things to question about the make-up of the grand jury that McGrath had put together. We discovered, for example, that one member of the grand jury was not even a resident of Jefferson County but lived in Hardin County and was best friends with a Beaumont deputy sher- iff. We filed that away for later reference.

The local judges disqualified themselves from sitting on this case; the judge assigned was Judge Pickett, from Midland. The star- tling part of this appointment was that the only contact that I had ever had with Judge Pickett was an occasion while representing the Oil Workers Union during a strike at Texaco. The judge entered an injunction against the local strike in Port Arthur by serving a union member who lived near the border of New Mexico. At that time an unincorporated association could be sued on behalf of all the mem- bers, no matter where he lived. I traveled to Midland and had a hearing to free my clients. They had ignored the judge's injunction and called the strike, despite his order. I was not successful. The judge overruled all my motions and sentenced all the members of the Port Arthur Workmen's Committee to jail for several days.

I was successful, however, in getting the state Supreme Court to overturn the judge's order and free my clients. Ultimately, after arguments, his injunction was tossed. My concern was how a seemingly anti-labor judge was going to treat me fairly. Fortunately, for me, with divine intervention, I happened to discuss the matter with a lawyer friend of mine while traveling on Southwest Airlines. I asked him if he knew the judge and told him of my concern about getting a fair hearing. He suggested that I shouldn't worry so much because this judge had retired and was no longer having to seek elected office in Midland, Texas. In fact, he told me that, in several criminal case hearings presided over by this judge in Houston, the judge was quick to take the prosecutors to task for not observing the strict letter of the law.

I then felt somewhat at ease in not trying to disqualify the judge but trusting that he would do the right thing. We went forward with preparing for the first hearing on the first indictment. Ultimately, the hearing was held, and the judge, I learned later, had commented to a fellow judge and friend of mine that he had never seen such a corrupt law enforcement group as he witnessed in Jefferson County. After discovering numerous irregularities and improper actions related to this grand jury, he dismissed all the charges.

I hoped this would end my travail, but undaunted, Jim McGrath and Calise Blanchard simply went forward with a second grand jury. Blanchard arrested Danny Lee approximately six or seven times, late at night. On the way to jail, he would tell Danny that all he needed to do was swear all the movie operation was mine, and he would dismiss everything against Danny.

The Second Grand Jury

The second grand jury was composed of fewer people connected with the Port Arthur Independent School District case. And I was able to get some information slipped out of the grand jury about what was being done. They abandoned the charge of lying to the grand jury but added at least one other charge claiming that I was involved with the delivery of drugs. The indictment claimed that I had promised two topless dancers cocaine to accompany me out of town and have sex. Fortunately, my investigator was able to locate the two dancers and discovered that prior to the first grand jury they had been arrested the night before and charged with felony resisting arrest. They were promised the charges against them would promptly be dropped if they testified as to any criminal conduct on my part. I had never met one of the dancers, but had been introduced to the other briefly, on one occasion when I stopped by

136

Danny Lee's house. I had never made any offer to either of those women.

We received numerous reports that the grand jury had interviewed many of my former employees and numerous ex-convicts claiming to know of criminal behavior on my part. One example that I learned about was a former client. He reported that he had been arrested and promised freedom if he could be of assistance. He first was induced by an undercover agent to accompany him on a trip to transport a large amount of drugs. He accompanied the undercover agent, supposedly on a flight to West Texas, where they landed and was promptly arrested by federal narcotics officers.

One of these officers had been the leading officer on a case I had handled where they claimed that my client had flown a plane load of drugs from Mexico to Tyler, Texas. During that trial, I caught the narcotics officer in a big lie when he claimed he had observed the plane; I clearly proved he had not. He was somewhat upset by being caught in the lie, and I could tell that he had it in for me. He turned out to be one of the officers arresting the former client. After the arrest, he told the client that he could go free if he would only tell him bad things about me. Fortunately, he didn't know any bad things but reported the incident to me. After Budd located the two dancers, it was imperative that we get statements from them about their falsified testimony. Budd had them flown from Galveston back to Port Arthur where they were interviewed by Tom Hanna. He obtained statements from them that indicated that their testimonies had been false and that they knew no such incident about me that they had testified to. McGrath and his accomplice, Calise Blanchard, were so infuriated by the fact that we had located their lying witnesses, that they indicted Budd, claiming that he had interfered with a grand jury investigation, and then threatened to indict Tom Hanna, our former district attorney.

A young man who worked in my Austin office worked out with an Austin detective. The detective asked this young man if he still worked for me. He affirmed that he did. During this conversation, the detective suggested that I should have my attorney contact the Austin Police Department and demand to see the first report of a home burglary that took place in Austin, Texas. Eventually we did get our hands on a police report which had been placed in a drawer of an Austin cop and replaced with a phony one. The facts were as follows. A lady called the Austin Police Department to report that two young women who were renting a bedroom from her had left for work. Shortly after they left for work at a topless joint in

Austin, she heard rummaging in their room. She took her pistol, stepped into the hallway, and was confronted by a short young man in a black sweater and ski mask holding a pistol. The intruder, in "typical burglar" fashion, took a stance with both hands on the gun and yelled at the lady, "freeze." She popped off a shot at him and retreated to her bedroom while he fled.

She called and reported the incident to the police who sent two policemen to investigate. After taking the report from the lady of the house, the two policemen drove up the street a short distance and stopped under a streetlight to complete their report. While doing their report, they received another call from the headquarters saying that the lady had called again saying the intruders were back in her home. They quickly backed up to the location of the alleged burglary, only to find a short young man in a black sweater, absent the ski mask, accompanied by three fellows in an automobile. After being arrested, the supposed burglar revealed that he was a deputy sheriff from Jefferson County and that the county was investigating a series of crimes supposedly committed by the local state senator. He had been searching the girls' room because he falsely believed they had incriminating photographs of me. He did, in fact, find cameras, took their negatives, only to find absolutely nothing about me. No charges were filed against the deputy sheriffs, but the incident was well documented and one which we were later able to present to a judge.

We learned of numerous other incidents where convicts or ex-convicts had been offered sentence reductions or even dismissal of chargest in exchange for any incriminating information about me. Fortunately, they were unsuccessful in locating any.

Mr. Tweedle, who became one of the star witnesses, while in another state, had been arrested for running a gambling joint. Later, it was discovered that Mr. Tweedle had employed a burglar to install a secret camera in the county attorney's office and then sent his wife to attempt to seduce the county attorney and get it on film. Again, fortunately, the county attorney discovered the camera and to escape further prosecution, Mr. Tweedle fled back to his hometown, Port Arthur, Texas.

During the second grand jury, a friend of mine asked a juror if they really had any evidence of a crime committed by me. The juror said, "Not really, but they thought they could get another indictment." He was right and a second indictment was issued. I was re-arrested, printed, photographed, and released on my own recognizance. When all was finally over, the court ordered all prints and evidence of my arrest to be destroyed or given to me!

The second hearing was held, and again, Judge Pickett presided. Several members of the grand jury were called as witnesses; one included the then editor of the *Beaumont Enterprise*. He had been foreman of the grand jury. He described the last meeting of the grand jury in which Calise Blanchard opened the doors to the grand jury room where they were greeted with copies of indictments against me sitting before each one's chair. Mr. Blanchard then proceeded to tell them that he had been a law enforcement officer for over twenty years, that he knew what it took to indict someone, and that he had provided more than enough. He said that, unless they handed down an indictment, he would get a judge to convene a court of inquiry to inquire into the lives of each member of the grand jury. When asked why such a procedure was held in the grand jury, the ex-foreman of the grand jury said it appeared that he was trying to intimidate them into handing down an indictment. The judge asked the ex-foreman if he was intimidated, and he confessed that in fact he was. The second indictment was dismissed.

The Third Grand Jury

A third grand jury was convened. McGrath, feeling the heat, disqualified himself and asked the state attorney general, Jim Maddox, to take over. Jim Maddox appointed an ex-district attorney from Galveston to run the grand jury. We received numerous reports of attempts by various deputies to intimidate the grand jury. Fortunately, none of these worked. By this time, it appeared that McGrath and Sheriff Culbertson, along with Calise Blanchard, had lost most of what little credibility they had in the county. This grand jury also indicted a deputy sheriff for subordination of perjury! Calise Blanchard was called but refused to testify. McGrath fired him, but the sheriff hired him as his number one deputy.

The final meeting of the grand jury was scheduled; all the local news media—newspapers and the three local TV stations— looked forward to it. It so happened that the date of the last grand jury meeting was on a date when Lieutenant Governor Bill Hobby had scheduled a visit to Port Arthur and Beaumont. During the day, I accompanied Governor Hobby on tours of Lamar and various other points of interest in the county. It was almost amusing in that we were followed by a parade of television vans and other news folks. Along with the caravan were two or three sheriff cars. What I learned later was that they had planned on getting a third indictment and arresting me while I was in the company of the lieutenant governor. They thought this would make great television and add to their cause to destroy me politically and personally. Fortunately, the day passed with no report. Late in the afternoon, we finished our tour with a reception for Governor Hobby at my home. We then got word that the grand jury had no-billed me with an overwhelming majority of the members of the grand jury voting for no-bill.

To say the least, we had a great celebration. As a matter of fact, several of my close friends and supporters were moved to tears in appreciation and relief.

I tell this story because I want at least my grandchildren, to know the truth about their grandfather. It also demonstrates what can happen to the law when enforcement officials are devoid of principles and have only their little vendettas to keep them going.

Post Script

Unfortunately, the no-billing did not end the adventure of my battle with law enforcement in Jefferson County or others who were similarly motivated. Two things were outstanding in my mind following the grand jury no-bill.

I received a call from a friend of mine named Danny Martin. Danny was a car dealer I had come to be friends with through Danny Doyle, my law partner. Danny called me to inform me that he had been contacted by Texas Rangers wanting to interview him about an incident that they said occurred in his office and involved me. Danny asked whether he should agree to the interview. I told him I had no qualms about him telling them anything that was true. Danny said he would consent to the interview if they promised not to ask him anything about his activities. After the interview, Danny called me to report that the Texas Ranger had told him they had a report, from some woman claiming to be my ex-girlfriend, that I had attended a party at his office and, supposedly, the party was interrupted by a topless dancer who announced that I had impregnated her. They told him that I became so enraged that I picked up a large metal stool and beat her to death. Further, the Rangers said that then I, Danny Martin, and a Black employee of Danny's drove down to McFaddin Beach, that they let me out with the body, and that I buried it on the beach. Apparently, the *Beaumont Enterprise* had paid for a bulldozer or some other heavy equipment to go to the alleged location of the burial and dig up approximately a half-mile of the beach. Fortunately, they did not uncover any remains or any bodies.

Later we discovered, after thorough investigation, with the help of Houston law enforcement, that the woman had swindled an elderly lady of Houston out of $25,000 and that she claimed that she had inside information about me and was going to publish a book that told all about our relationship. The book was never written and the woman, it turned out, had never met me in person. She was sentenced to several days in jail for filing false police reports.

The next incident included a phone call to Beverly while I was in Austin. The caller announced that he had an incriminating video of me and that, unless we forked over $20,000, he was going to publish it in Jefferson County. She told him she had to talk to me first; he said he would call back. He also indicated, over the phone, that he knew where we lived and he was not that far away. In between phone calls, when she could not locate me, she contacted our son, Allen, who came rushing over. When the second call came in, Allen believed he knew where the individual was, dashed out of the house, and drove to a nearby shopping center where he saw an individual talking on a pay phone—this was before everyone had a cell. Approaching the second pay phone booth, beside the one being used, he asked the fellow if he had some change. He pretended to talk on the phone, but Beverly could hear Allen talking to the guy. Later, Allen reported that the guy was pretty big but that he thought he could have taken him if not for his companion, who was waiting in the car. Allen tried to follow him when he left but was unable to. It later turns out that the guy was about 6'6" and weighed about 270 pounds. Allen at the time weighed about 135. I appreciate his view that he could have taken him, but I doubt it seriously and am pleased that he didn't try.

The guy continued to make threatening calls. Eventually, after we set several traps trying to catch him, he called while I was at the office. I had a tape recorder attached to the phone. I asked him what kind of videos he intended to publish about me. He said it was a video of me having sex with young women. I couldn't resist cracking a joke, telling him that it had to be an old, old video, to which he replied that I was an SOB and that, if I didn't take it seriously, he would kill me and my whole family. I then took the recording I made over the phone to the local Texas Ranger who immediately recognized the voice.

He went to the fellow's house with other law enforcement, and upon opening the door, the man said, "If you are here about that video, I don't know anything about it." He was arrested and found to be an ex-football player who was having serious mental problems. He ended up pleading guilty to extortion and received a probated sentence that included mental treatment. He later violated his probation and was sentenced to prison. A couple of years later, Beverly had an older-than-average student tell her that the night she had received the calls, this individual had come to his brother's house wanting a gun, saying that he was going to kill the Parkers.

The third weird instance was an occasion when Beverly and I were about to have dinner at the Schooner. I got a call before we left that a reporter for the *Beaumont Enterprise* had been shot by an assassin who had crawled through his bedroom window. He said he believed it was me getting revenge for bad stories written about me by the *Beaumont Enterprise*. Greeted with this knowledge, we went to dinner anyway although we were sick to think that the accusations would start all over again.

We were greeted by the waitress, who told us she was married to a Beaumont detective who had reported a weird incident to her that very evening. He had been called to investigate the shooting of *The Beaumont Enterprise* reporter. Upon investigation, he noticed a blood trail from the bedroom and out the back door, which he followed. Upon checking under the back steps of the house, he found an old "Saturday night special" covered with blood, apparently hidden there by the reporter. It turns out the reporter was having mental problems himself, shot himself in the head, made up the story about me, and hid the pistol.

McGrath quit, and the sheriff was defeated in his next election. The legislature also changed the rules about how grand juries are selected. Now grand juries are not handpicked by a judge but randomly selected as are other jurors.

One overall result of all the publicity concerning my indictment and various hearings was that the system of grand jury selection was reformed in Jefferson County. It was obvious the grand juries in my case had been hand-selected by law enforcement, some of which appeared to have been corrupt. Now, in Jefferson County and probably most counties of Texas, grand jury membership is selected on a random basis much the same way that regular juries are selected.

I am sure there are other stories, most of which I have hopefully forgotten, putting the whole mess behind me. Lesson learned— "You can get in trouble, even when you have done nothing wrong." Be loyal to friends but take great care when you get close to them.

Part V: Practicing Law

Prologue

For more than 60 years of plying my trade of practicing law, I am absolutely convinced that, if there are lawyers with a more varied practice than I have had, I have seldom, if ever, heard of any of them. My practice has gone from the small claims court to the Supreme Court of the United States and almost everything in between. It has involved short and lengthy trials, criminal and civil matters as well as international law and lobbying the legislature and Congress. I have met some interesting people along the way and handled some unusual cases by anyone's standards. I have decided to catalog them in a series of essays about various cases in which I have participated. In some of the cases, although the facts are real and based on real life, I have altered the names of some to protect the guilty as well as some of the innocent.

Water Supply

Handling civil tort claims, death investigations, and over 350 court martials involving everything from murder, robbery, AWOL, desertion, and various other crimes and offenses more than prepared me for the private practice of law in a small to medium size town. When I launched my law practice, I was well prepared for one of the most varied law practices ever known.

My first federal court case went all the way through the appeal process, ultimately requiring me to file briefs with the United States Supreme Court. Although I had hundreds of cases which would make good stories, some I remember more than others. The longest case I ever participated in was the case involving the Fredeman family. Captain and Sydelis Fredeman were great citizens and benefactors of the city of Port Arthur. Mrs. Fredeman, probably more than anyone before or since, was responsible for seeing that worthwhile civic endeavors were adequately funded. The Fredeman fortune was made when Captain Fredeman started a towing company during WWII, which grew into a very profitable industry. Later on, under Captain Fredeman's tutelage the Port Arthur Towing Company had grown substantially and includued a subsidiary called Mid-Stream Fueling. Mid-Stream Fueling supplied diesel fuel to tug boats plying the intracoastal waterway. Mid-Stream used a small tug and barge which could transfer fuel to larger tugboats while underway. This meant the larger boats did not lose time as they moved cargo up or down the intracoastal waterway. The problem arose when a former employee of Mid-Stream went into business for himself and contacted federal authorities claiming that Mid-Stream was systematically stealing fuel from its customers. The accusation, which later proved to be true, was that Mid-Stream had installed a reverse flow valve on its fueler to return ten percent of whatever was pumped through back into its own barge, thereby cheating every customer out of ten percent of what they paid for.

The feds responded eventually by indicting the corporation, the three Fredeman siblings, and many of their employees with a RICO charge. RICO was a federal offense designed to combat the Mafia. The standard for RICO basically was proving that five people or more had combined in a criminal enterprise to violate the law. I and several attorneys were employed to defend the various defendants involved in the case. Two of my clients were mid-level management employees who were the go-betweens between top management and on the water employees.

Among those hired was a well-known criminal defense lawyer in Texas, Racehorse Haynes. One of my greatest remembrances of the trial, which lasted almost six months in federal court, was the time I was able to win a $100 bet from Racehorse concerning happenings within the trial. Our investigator had revealed to us that one star witness for the government, a former employee unhappy with the company because he had been forced to work overtime on a weekend, retaliated by defecating in a freshwater tank of the supply boat that he ran out to the oil rigs in the Gulf. Almost every lawyer in the case argued that this witness's action was not admissible, particularly because we were under orders from the court to approach with any outside bad conduct that we intended to introduce about the government witnesses.

Haynes and I had a friendly bet as to whether I could persuade the judge to allow the admission of the conduct of this government witness. All the lawyers had established the order in which we would question government witnesses. I was to go first, Haynes last. When the government presented this witness, I began questioning him with routine cross examination and then, I asked to approach the bench. I informed the judge I intended to offer that this witness was spiteful against his employer and that he had once defecated in a fresh water supply tank. Of course, the U.S. attorney vigorously objected, asking the judge, "What, if anything, your honor, does it have to do with the issue of stealing fuel?"

The judge looked at me and asked, "Yeah, what does it have to do with anything in this case?"

I looked at the judge, an old East Texas boy who had grown up in the piney woods, and asked him whether he would trust anything said by someone who would "crap" in his drinking water. The judge thought for a minute, chuckled, and then announced that he was allowing the testimony. I confronted the witness and asked him whether or not it was true that he was so spiteful, mean, and vindicative that he "defecated" in the freshwater tank of one of his company's supply boats. He vigorously denied that he had ever done such a thing. I looked him in the eye and asked, "Are you telling me under oath that you never crapped in the water supply of a supply boat?" "Oh yeah," he said, "I done that." Thereby I secured my $100 bet with Haynes.

Practicing Law Can Be Dangerous

After returning from the Navy, because of my father's activities with the union in various leadership capacities, I was called on to represent the local Oil Chemical & Atomic Workers. Shortly after I began to represent them, a serious strike was called at one of the chemical plants in Orange, Texas. The plant was located on a strip of land where Dupont and other chemical companies were located, thereby giving that strip of land the name Chemical Row. The strike went on for some time and those involved became very embittered. The union guys began to get somewhat violent. On numerous occasions, I was required to bail union members out for having physically attacked or beaten-up strike breakers. On one occasion, as I was traveling to the Orange County Court House to do such a duty, I had to pass the location of the picket line in front of this chemical company. As I approached, I noticed cars doing U-turns ahead of me and heading back in the opposite direction and a plume of black smoke billowing from what appeared to be near the front gate of the chemical company. As I got near enough to see, I saw an automobile overturned and on fire.

I was somewhat chagrined that I had warned my striking clients on numerous occasions to refrain from violence because it could bring about serious consequences, such as enjoining the picket line itself. As I pulled up near the scene of the burning car and jumped from my car, I approached a little shack that was called the "picket shack" and began to berate the leader of the union about causing such violence near the picket line. He started laughing loudly which infuriated me in that I believed that he was ignoring my advice. When I asked him what was so funny, he simply said that there had been no violence but they had purchased a junk car for $50, turned it over, and set it on fire, giving the impression that they might have attacked a strike breaker attempting to drive through the picket line. He said, "It worked!" I am sure it did in view of the fact of the number of cars that approached the gate, did a U-turn, and fled in the opposite direction.

This strike was particularly interesting and turned out to be somewhat dangerous to me. Some of the strikers decided to engage in more violence. They were able to acquire a stash of dynamite from one of the striker's girlfriend's relatives in Louisiana. The dynamite in Louisiana was used regularly to blow up stumps to clear land. Unfortunately for the strikers, they knew little or nothing about how to handle dynamite. As a result, when they attempted to blow up a major pipeline headed to the chemical company, they only succeeded in blowing a huge hole in the ground causing absolutely no damage to the pipeline. The explosion, however, caused a lot of talk in Orange, Texas. An article in *The Orange Leader,* the local newspaper, claimed that what they were doing was so dangerous that they could have caused harm to property and citizens of Orange County.

Although the explosion caused no serious risk to anyone's property or person, the feeling in Orange among anti-strikers was that they were dangerous individuals who wreaked havoc in the quiet city of Orange. They were indicted, but upon the trial, I pulled out a provision in the law requiring more than simply an accomplice testimony to convict anyone of a serious crime. The only witness available to the state in this case was the girlfriend who in fact was considered an accomplice in that she had assisted in obtaining the dynamite. The Texas Rangers acquired her testimony by threatening to have her children taken away from her, and therefore, she gave a full confession. Unfortunately, there were no other witnesses to the state to corroborate the girlfriend's testimony. When the hearing came before the district court, there was no seating room in the courtroom. The newspaper was holding forth awaiting a serious punishment verdict. But all those folks were disappointed when the judge ruled that he had to dismiss the charges.

To say the least, I was not treated very kindly in the newspaper, but what followed was somewhat scary. Shortly after the hearing and dismissal of my clients' charges, I began to receive notes from an anonymous source telling me that I would be shot and killed were I to travel over the Orange bridge into Orange County at any time in the future. It was one of the few times in my career I felt the need to arm myself, which I did by carrying one of my pistols in my briefcase.

Near Miss

Many years into my law practice when it was located on Stadium Road, an ex-convict named Henry called on me to be his lawyer. Henry was a tall muscular fellow who had been twice convicted of burglary and theft. Henry claimed to be reformed and had established a popular drive-in restaurant on Procter Street near where Beverly and I lived at the time. Several times Henry was arrested and called me for representation. Henry was usually arrested because he had a statewide reputation as being an expert safe burglar. So, any time there was a safe burglary in Port Arthur, the cops would routinely pick up Henry for questioning just to see whether or not he might have been the appropriate object of investigation. Usually, by the time I reached the police station, they had satisfied themselves that Henry was not the person committing the crime, and in most cases, Henry would be released the moment I got there.

Henry mistakenly believed that I had such great sway or respect with the police that they would automatically dismiss him as a suspect anytime I appeared on the scene. Henry had a saying that he loved to brag to his friends about me. Henry's saying was that, when I arrived at the police station where he was in custody, I would ask the police if they believed in the "hereafter," and if they said "yes," then I would reply that I am here after Henry, let him go. Henry was such an expert at dealing with locks, I once challenged him to enter my office without the benefit of a key. In less than two minutes, with no key, Henry came through the door to demonstrate his ability.

Early one morning, way before dawn, I received a call from Henry's wife who had been, at the time of meeting Henry, a lady of questionable repute from Galveston. She told me that she and Henry had been out on the town, had quite a bit to drink, and when they returned home, in a fit of jealousy, Henry had slapped her around and threatened to kill her. She claimed she had fled in her nightgown about a block to a doctor's home who gave her shelter.

She told me that all she would like is to be free to return to Galveston and escape Henry's wrath. She asked that I call Henry. She believed that Henry would listen to reason if I imparted it.

I got Henry on the phone and told him that being fearful of a third conviction which could glean him life in prison, he would be better off to de-escalate the matter with his wife and to let her leave if that is what she wanted to do. Henry said that he would like to at least talk to her before that. I arranged for a 7:00 meeting at my office, which was right across the street from the doctor's residence where the wife had fled. Henry appeared as did his wife in her nightgown. As Henry walked in, he drew back as if to slug his wife when I cautioned him, that he had promised me that he would behave himself while in my office. During the conversation, Henry vowed that he had no further use for his wife and that he would be glad for her to be gone. I asked if he would behave himself while she gathered her belongings and departed. He assured me that that would be the case.

The wife asked if I would drive her to the bus station, which I agreed to do. Henry and his wife's residence was about a block away from my office so Henry drove home, and I, along with his wife, followed. When we reached their home, Henry opened the door and stepped inside, the wife followed, and by the time I got through the door, Henry had "doe-popped" her on the jaw, knocking her into a flip across the living room. I jumped between the two of them to try to deescalate the matter when Henry reached around the corner of an adjoining door, pulled out a single-barrel twelve-gauge shotgun, cocked it, stuck it in my belly, and said, "You're in my home now, I can shoot you dead."

Well, being young, stupid, and overly brave at the time, in anger I looked at Henry, saying, "You promised to behave yourself. And if you don't put that damn gun down, I am going to turn you in to the cops and see that you do life in the pen."

Henry relaxed his grip on the gun, but said, "You need to get out of my house." I gladly obliged. However, before the time I reached the outside, steps away from my car, I realized what I had done, said, and what could have been. My knees got so shaky I barely made it to the car.

I put this down as a lesson learned and returned to my office. Henry let the wife go and all was well.

But as it turns out, I hadn't learned my lesson. Not much later, a lady came into my office because she had taken up with a husband who was very abusive. It turns out the husband was unemployed and a drunk. He had beaten the lady up so badly that her face looked like it had been used for a soccer ball. She asked that I file for a divorce for her in that the husband was not working and sponging off her—as well as abusing her on a regular basis. She said, "You have to be careful because he is crazy."

I said, "Well tell that big boy to come down and see if he would try slapping a full-grown man who has some defensive skills."

She said, "No, don't do that, just file for my divorce."

A few days later, the lady returned to my office, still bearing the scars of her beating, and demanded that I dismiss the divorce. Again, I issued a challenge that I asked her to send on to her husband to come challenge me and see how it turned out. She, then, told me to drop the divorce, "The guy is crazy and he will either kill or try to kill you and me both." I responded to her that such boasts usually by spouses involved in a divorce were just talk. Nevertheless, she kept insisting that I drop the divorce, which I did.

A week after dropping the divorce, however, she called to tell me that she had been at a club in Groves, Texas, called the Black Cat, simply sitting at the bar near a young man when the husband walked in and full of jealous rage, shot and killed the male customer of the establishment. I have to put that down as another lesson learned about young lawyers with bravado. They risk not growing into old lawyers with no bravado.

The End of Sweet Black Walker

I received a call at my office and was confronted over the phone by a woman who seemed to be irritated beyond measure. She claimed that her husband had been jailed for killing a burglar in their own home and that I should go and see about him at the lock up at the Port Arthur Police Station. I did so and encountered Lynn who was the husband in question. It seemed that not only Lynn but his wife and three other relatives had been charged and later indicted for the murder of "Sweet Black Walker."

Although the standards have changed, at the time, I was able to represent all five defendants together in one trial. As I proceeded to investigate the facts underlying the charges against my clients, several interesting things were revealed. It seems that Lynn and his family took a trip to visit other relatives in Louisiana. Upon returning, they discovered their home had been burglarized. Suspiciously, I learned that Lynn and his family were probably dealing in small amounts of marijuana and the object of the burglary was to discover and rob them of their stash of weed. Though no marijuana was found at the time of the break in, the burglar proceeded to deprive them of their brand-new Susi stereo system and some other electronic gear.

149

Being unhappy about the discovery that their home had been violated, Lynn and his relatives set about to discover the name of the perpetrator. This effort led them to Gillam Park, a large circular park that had originally been planned to be the center of town and was located not far from their residence. Lynn armed himself with an antique Colt .45 automatic stuffed in his waistband and proceeded to Gillam Circle where they found a juvenile delinquent well known for his involvement with thieves and other would-be criminals. After approaching the teenage delinquent, they captured him and took him to their home. The delinquent was encouraged to tell the truth because Lynn and his accomplices placed a rope around his neck, pitched it over one of the rafters in the garage, and hoisted the delinquent up until he was persuaded to reveal the name of the person who had made off with their property. That person was known as "Sweet Black Walker," a well-known thief, burglar, and dope dealer in the city.

Armed with the identity of the perpetrator, Lynn and his crew proceeded to locate Sweet Black a few nights later in a bar located on Seventh Street in Port Arthur. At gun point, they escorted Sweet Black to their home, confronted him about his malfeasance, clubbed him over the head with the .45, and shot him dead as he lay on the floor. Unfortunately, Lynn was later sentenced to five years for manslaughter, the other four defendants accepted probation as their punishment for manslaughter. The technicality that convicted them all, however, seemed to be that, although Sweet Black was killed as a burglar in the home of Lynn, the killing and the burglary occurred a little over a week apart.

Sly Plan in Child Custody

Although I have handled numerous child custody disputes, some still are unique in my memory. In one case, I represented a gentleman seeking custody of his children and it was a jury trial. Both parties introduced all the bad things they could about the opposing party which ultimately caused the jury to send a question out of the jury room to the judge asking whether they could remove the children from both parents. Ultimately my guy won.

Fast forward a few years and my client, Jim, had remarried, and he was required to share visitation with his ex. Unfortunately, his ex-wife managed to become great friends with the new and younger wife. The ex-wife lured the new wife into accompanying her on a Wednesday night, girls-only outing. They traveled to a dance hall in Beaumont where the present wife became enamored with an ex-convict who apparently was a great dancer and a rather handsome dude. After several visits to the dance hall, the ex-wife suggested to the present wife that there was a way that she could have a tryst with her newfound acquaintance at the dance hall. She suggested that she would simply drop them off at her house and ride around for an hour or two. They could have their romantic evening together, unknown to Jim, the husband, who was babysitting all the children. Since it sounded like a good idea to the new wife, she agreed, and the ex-wife dropped her and her would-be lover off at the ex-wife's home. As soon as they became ensconced in the ex-wife's house, the ex-wife immediately traveled to the home of Jim, telling him to gather the children because she had something exciting to show him about what a slut his new wife was. She took them to her home, quietly unlocked the door, and had them walk in on the new wife in bed with her newfound boyfriend.

The ex-wife then used this as a basis of seeking to overturn Jim's custody of the children, saying that he had entrusted his children to an unprincipled slut, and that unprincipled sluts are usually bad for the children. Fortunately for Jim, the trick didn't work, and he maintained custody of his children. It did have a quieting effect on the amount of visitation that was allowed by the court thereafter.

Don't Mess with Old Men

I received a call from a distraught wife whose husband, Bill, had been arrested for shooting and killing another elderly gentleman. Bill at the time was 79; the gentleman slain by Bill was 80. It seems that the deceased owned a vacant lot directly across the street and across from the driveway of Bill and his wife. The deceased apparently took great delight in manicuring the property of his vacant lot. Not only did he mow more than once a week during summertime growth but edged the various curbsides and other matters by hand. For several years, Bill complained that the deceased hampered his ability to enter his driveway because of where the deceased parked his vehicle.

Bill had been a champion tennis player in his youth and continued his efforts to play a decent game of tennis well into his 70s. Clearly his abilities were declining due to the symptoms of old age, a source of frustration to Bill in that he seriously felt that he was losing his manhood. On one occasion, when returning from the YMCA where he had exercised, he had difficulty navigating into his driveway because of the location of the deceased gentleman's vehicle.

Bill shouted across the street to the gentleman asking to please move his vehicle and not park it behind the drive, making it difficult to enter. The gentleman simply laughed and said, "Well that's a loading zone, can't you tell?"

As Bill described to me later, he said, "I just couldn't take it anymore." Bill, who was an army veteran, went into his home, retrieved his army carbine he somehow had kept, came out of his house, pointed the gun at his neighbor and demanded again that he move his vehicle. The gentleman owning the vacant lot simply laughed, rose, and gave the single middle-finger salute to Bill.

Bill fired one shot which was not very accurate. At the time, he was supporting himself with his three-legged cane in one hand and attempting to aim and shoot the carbine with his other hand and arm. After the first shot, Bill again demanded that the car be moved, and the neighbor responded with a middle-finger salute. Bill fired again. The third time Bill made his demand and got the third salute, he fired and struck the gentleman in the heart.

With these facts, I was committed to defend Bill in court. After I described all the circumstances and had Bill testify, I pointed out that he not only was a veteran, he was a good citizen, never even having a parking ticket or any other minor violation of the law; the judge gave Bill a fairly light sentence of three years. Bill was in very poor health, however, and Texas had recently adopted a statute that allowed a judge, after sentence, to reduce the sentence if the sentence was less than five years. Bill had gone to jail and was having a terrible time because he was so severely arthritic. He was spending considerable time and the state's money because of his ailments. After making this known to the judge, I argued to the judge that in fact it was not really murder but suicide on the part of the deceased. Anyone who could defy someone pointing a loaded weapon at him and shooting the finger, especially in Southeast Texas, was asking to be killed. Bill only accommodated the gentleman. My argument worked with the judge and reduced the sentence to four months, and he was released from jail.

In only a few weeks after my adventure with Bill shooting his would-be neighbor, I received an additional call from another wife whose husband had been arrested and charged with capital murder for having slain two of his neighbors. Upon investigation, I learned that Sam, who lived in the area known as Port Acres, had not only shot two of his neighbors with a pistol but killed them good by pumping two shots of buck shot into each neighbor as they lay dying in a ditch near the front of his home.

The whole affair came about because the neighborhood in which Sam's home was located was a subdivision originally created by the father of the lady who lived next door. Even after Sam had moved into the neighborhood, the mailbox of the neighbor was still placed in such a manner that Sam could not navigate from the street down the side of his house to gain access to his backyard. After the neighbors denied Sam's numerous requests to move the mailbox, the issue became so controversial that the local priest, the county judge, the local postmaster, and several others were called on to mediate the dispute between the neighbors. All of the efforts failed.

Therefore, one early morning, Sam's wife rose to note that Sam had gathered his chainsaw, sawed down the offending mail-box, and tossed it into the front yard of his neighbor. Two days later, to Bill's chagrin, the neighbor's husband and his brother-in-law repositioned another mailbox in the very same spot. Sam went outside and jokingly said, "Go ahead, I can cut them down faster than you can put them up."

According to Sam, when I interviewed him, he said that the neighbor said, "Go ahead you old son-of-a-bitch, but if you cut this one down, it will be the last thing you ever cut down." My client said that, with that reply, he was convinced he absolutely had to kill both men. Sam returned to his house, retrieved a 22 automatic pistol, and by the time he emerged from the house, the offending wife was accompanying her husband and his brother-in-law near the mailbox. Sam popped off a shot in the direction of the wife who immediately fled. He then shot each of the men one time. As he described it, "They were lying in the ditch writhing around in pain." He then explained to me that he had always heard that if you shoot someone, you better kill them because they will eventually seek revenge and kill you. Sam returned to his house, came back with his 12-gauge riot shotgun, and pumped two buck shots into each of the gentlemen he had just shot.

I later learned that the police, upon arriving, found Sam perched on his front porch calmly smoking a cigarette. As the police approached him, he asked, "Are they dead?" The policeman expressed that he did not know, that they were being looked after by the EMTs. My client's reply was, "Damn, it would be a shame to go to the penitentiary and not have killed the bastards."

Sam related to me the story of one of his pet cat who had apparently offended the neighbor by tracking over the neighbor's car and leaving footprints. To keep the peace at the time, Sam had the cat euthanized. In telling the story, big tears welled up in his eyes, showing sympathy for having to kill the cat.

Unfortunately, he had no similar sympathy for the two men he had killed. I later also learned that Sam had obstruction in his carotid arteries that influenced his mental process. I sought the advice of a psychiatrist and, in a motion to reduce the penalty of the crime for which he was charged, revealed his reduced mental capacity. Even though the psychiatrist testified to such, Judge Gist refused to accept the motion and later told me that he felt he would probably be reversed on appeal. When I presented his wife from the witness stand to tell of Sam's delusions, she testified that, after the killing, he seemed to be in a better humor than he had been for months.

When the district attorney cross-examined her, she became overwrought. She fainted and fell face forward to the floor from the witness stand.

The jury gave Sam 20-25 years for murder. Of course, I appealed and felt sure the case would be reversed. Unfortunately, in a way Sam was never convicted because he died of a serious stroke while in jail. Unfortunately for the wife, the story did not end. The heirs of the two gentlemen slain by Sam filed a civil suit and attempted to gain all the property of Sam's widow. Although there was little hope for an adequate defense, I was able to work out a settlement wherein Sam's wife was allowed to live in the home for the rest of her life. Hers and Sam's estates would satisfy the judgement when she died.

Another prevalent phenomenon I discovered in the practice of law was that, often, the client would relate to you early on what he or she thinks is the best way to present their case. The same is certainly true of those accused of a crime who always have some theory of why they should not be convicted. The most unique proposed strategy, however, that I ever encountered was a client who thought he could extract himself from jail by confessing to multiple murders which he did not commit.

I was approached by a Port Arthur family to represent a member of their family who had been indicted in Harris County for attempted murder that came about because of a savage beating of his estranged wife.

Although having been estranged for a while, they continued to talk via telephone and eventually agreed to try to unite after which he treated his wife to wine and dinner at a fancy restaurant in Houston. Very shortly after dinner the wife confessed that she had had numerous affairs with other men during the period of their

154

separation. This news enraged my client. He stopped the car, jerked her out, beat her savagely, and left her unconscious beside the road. Because of the severity of the injuries, the female judge decided that a bond in excess of a million dollars was appropriate for the circumstances. Of course, neither the client nor the family could afford a bond of that size. The client languished in jail. After receiving a small down payment on the fees I quoted, I set about attempting to help this gentleman. Unfortunately, I quickly discovered, after interviewing the client and discussing the matter with the prosecutor, that my client had not only been accused of the severe beating of his estranged wife but that, during his stay in jail, he had voluntarily confessed to the murders of a family who had been killed in a home invasion/robbery in Harris County.

The confession came about because my client had been locked up in cells with several other accused felons and overheard them discussing the fact that, after robbing a family, they killed the family and set fire to the home to cover up the evidence. My client smuggled a note to one of the jailers and eventually was interviewed by the district attorney, relating all he had heard. On the demand of my client, he was transferred out of the cell block to a more secure lockup in the Harris County jail where he also demanded special privileges such as having a television installed in his cell along with special meals. Being angered by the county's refusal to afford him the luxuries he demanded, he then decided he no longer wanted to testify and smuggled another note to the jailer saying, "I am the one who killed the family." Of course, this enraged the district attorney who was counting on my client's testimony to convict those who had really committed the murder.

I was therefore faced with the challenge to not only defend the severe beating of the wife but to also see what I could do to clear up the matter where he had confessed to murder. After only a short investigation, I was able to prove to the satisfaction of the court and to the district attorney that my client could not have committed the murders because we were able to prove he was not even in the state of Texas at the time the robbery, murder, and arson occurred.

We then returned to the issue of his problems and the size of his bond. I was able to get his bond reduced to a reasonable amount, which allowed the family to scrape up enough money to free him from jail. I continued my representation and persuaded the judge that although the injuries were serious, that it had been largely brought about by the estranged wife simply baiting him and daring him to do anything about it. As a matter of fact, I eventually was able to persuade the judge to agree to a plea of guilty and probation with severe restraints on my client after being released. Believe it or not, on the date we were to enter the plea and receive probation, my client failed to show up to take advantage of his probation.

Another bad end to the case was that I never received my fee.

All Kinds of Clients

If the practice of law as a profession is anything, it is one of the most interesting ways to make a living. You meet all kinds of people and are faced with many types of challenges. Particularly when you begin the practice of law, it opens new vistas. As a beginning lawyer struggling for clients, I accepted almost any opportunity to practice. Among those opportunities was one offered by the presiding judge in Jefferson County who appointed me to be lawyer for people who were indigent, faced with a sanity hearing. Some of the most interesting people I ever met accompanied this adventure. Among those I represented was one declaring herself to be queen of the world, and another claimed that God had appointed him to be manager of the Texaco Refinery in Port Arthur. Consequently, he marched into the plant manager's office and ordered him out. Others had some interesting quirks that led them to sanity hearings. A merchant seaman whose home nestled beside the ship channel in Port Arthur claimed that he received radio communications continually from ships at sea. His fixation on communication resulted in his having a telephone installed in every room in his home, an act not favored by his wife who filed a complaint leading to the insanity hearing.

The biggest problem in representing people whose sanity is questioned is getting them to listen to good advice or giving you facts upon which you can rest a defense. I was once appointed to represent a gentleman whose girlfriend had filed such a complaint. Unfortunately, although it takes a medical diagnosis to support a sanity hearing, most doctors at the time would not bother to take the time to come to the courthouse and testify. Most cases were simply based on medical records presented by the county attorney. Another problem in most sanity hearings was the fact that, to calm the object of the sanity hearing, the patient would be given calming drugs and generally did not act out or demonstrate the conduct which led to the hearing.

On one occasion, my client appeared in court well-dressed, very calm, and not offering much in the way of facts I could base a defense on. However, on the other side, there was little evidence of his lack of compos mentis. Like most relatives and loved ones filing complaints, they were very reluctant to take the stand, look their loved one in the eye, and claim they were mentally incompetent and should be constrained to treatment without their permission. This case was no different. The girlfriend who lived in a mobile home with my client was so reluctant she offered little, if anything, indicating the sanity question of my client. When the county attorney rested his case, the judge asked me if I wanted to present evidence, firmly believing, and correctly so, that not enough evidence had been presented to justify finding my client not sane. I declined to offer any evidence. Unfortunately, contrary to my advice, my client rose quickly and demanded of the judge to be heard. The county's attorney quickly said, "I object!"

The judge looked at the county attorney, and said, "No you don't!" and then allowed my client to take the stand.

He said that he would like to speak to the court; he stood in an angry manner, pointing his finger at his girlfriend, who had just testified and demanded in a loud, angry voice, "What the hell did you do with my Bull Durm that you stole?" He went on with a rambling discourse about how his girlfriend had deprived him of one of his worldly pleasures—that is smoking his own, "roll your own" cigarettes. He was deemed to be in need of serious mental treatment.

Free at Last

Losing the election was certainly disappointing but brought about a feeling of relief. Living the life of politics for 32 years takes a toll; I missed a lot with my children such as school plays, little league games, piano recitals, and other occasions normally attended by parents. I had become accustomed to the burden of having to sit through boring club events and attending dozens of chambers of commerce banquets, most of which seemed to be the same throughout my multi-county senatorial district. I had done it so long that by the time I was halfway through my senate term, it seemed like a normal thing to do all the time. Someone opined it was like the old story about the man who every day picked up a baby elephant when it was born and having done it so often, he didn't realize how heavy the load was.

Leaving office I found new freedom, not the least of which was only having to work a five-day workweek and enjoying work-free weekends.

As soon as it was clear that I would no longer be required to spend senate time, I began to be approached about the possibility of becoming a lobbyist. It seemed to be a natural path. I have often been asked, "How does one become a lobbyist?" I always explain to the inquirer that the first and main requirement to become a lob-byist is obtaining a client. Fortunately, after the end of my political career as an officeholder, there was no shortage of perspective clients. Other skills needed to be a lobbyist involve the ability to raise campaign cash, know the rules of both the House and Senate, know the customs honored by the legislature, and have a good relation-ship with the lieutenant governor, speaker of the house, governor, and other members of the legislature. Being friends and former colleagues with officeholders such as the land commissioner, comp-troller, and secretary-of-state is also very helpful in establishing yourself as a competent lobbyist.

Fortunately, my law practice took off to the extent that I was able to open a second law office in Austin along with my office in Port Arthur. Some of my first clients were the Texas State Troopers Association, the city of Port Arthur, the Texas Trial Lawyers, and Coastal States Corporation headed by my friend and benefactor Oscar S. Wyatt, Jr. Having been freed from the responsibility of public service made it much easier to earn a living. I had often told folks that serving in the legislature cost me money. I truly believed it to be so, but I had no proof. It did, however, prove to be true. By the fourth month of my newfound freedom, my income had already reached four times the monthly income of what I had made my last year in office.

The Liberia Story

I had represented Oscar Wyatt, a wealthy oilman and CEO of the Coastal States Corporation, for many years. Wyatt at the time, apparently, had a contract with the nation of Liberia to explore for uranium. Wyatt was also working with the president of Liberia at the time to establish registration for commercial cargo aircraft in Liberia. Liberia was known worldwide for cheap regis-tration of sea-going vessels. Wyatt told me that the president of Liberia had complained to him that even though Liberia was a great friend of the U.S., it had been pretty much ignored. Wyatt suggested to him that he knew a lawyer in Texas who was also tuned into politics. Shortly thereafter, Wyatt arranged to transport me from Houston to Monrovia, Liberia, to meet with the president.

As we circled the airport in Monrovia in Wyatt's airplane, a commercial jet liner for Delta Airlines appeared to be seeking to land at the same time. The controller, however, put the commercial airliner on hold as we landed.

Upon exiting the plane, we were greeted by a military escort standing at attention on each side of a red carpet. We followed the red carpet to an awaiting lounge where I was introduced to President Tolbert, president of Liberia along with presidents of three other African nations.

After attending a very formal dinner which included President Tolbert and members of his cabinet, I was employed to be Liberia's lawyer in the United States. I was required to register with the State Department as a foreign agent and report in detail what funds I had received from Liberia and how they were spent. This was required quarterly. I made several trips to Liberia, all of which were very pleasant. I was royally entertained by the president and members of his cabinet while making me thoroughly familiar with the activities and economy of the country.

One of the principal industries in Liberia was the rubber plantations, the largest of which were owned and operated by American owned corporations. The local economy depended primarily on agricultural endeavors, the main one of which was rice fields. Coming from Southeast Texas, I was very familiar with rice farming. I discovered that in Liberia it was very different. What was called "cleared fields" in Liberia were not the cleared fields I had known but fields in which large trees had been cut down, leaving the stumps in the fields. This, of course, made it very difficult to use heavy equipment to harvest the rice. Harvesting was done mostly by women. I was able to witness one of the rice harvests while I was there. The harvesters were females dressed only from the waist down, carrying small knives and aprons. They would walk through the field, cutting the heads off the rice plants and dropping them in their aprons as they went. They also sang as they went along twenty or thirty abreast, seemingly making harvesting a very pleasant operation for them.

The government had attempted to diversify their crops by handing out small parcels of land in which Liberians could farm a small crop of rice and plant palm oil trees. Unfortunately, without patience, most of the beneficiaries of the land grants could not persist in their agricultural efforts and soon sold off the parcels, not wanting to wait the length of time it would take for the palm oil trees to mature. I was able to give some assistance to the agricultural efforts in Liberia through my connection with the Texas A&M rice facility in China, Texas, and through the University of Alabama.

I was also successful in substantially increasing America's foreign aid to Liberia, primarily through the help and efforts of my old friend Congressman Charlie Wilson, who at the time was chairman of the appropriate committee of Congress.

On one of my visits, I had some spare time, having finished a meeting with the president and his cabinet somewhat early. I decided to take a walking tour of Monrovia accompanied by Augustus Bodah, a young man assigned to me as my guide and "gofer" while in Liberia. While awaiting a traffic signal, I noticed that standing nearby was a lady with a dishpan on her head filled with lobsters. Two of the lobsters were dangling over the edge of the pan. I held up my camera and pointed to her. She smiled as though inviting me to take her picture, so I snapped the photograph.

Across the street was a gentleman, well dressed in a western style suit. He quickly approached me and said, "You need to give me your camera. You just took an unauthorized photograph of that lady and that's illegal." I told him she looked like she wanted her picture taken. He then told me that I would either have to give him my camera or be taken to the police station. By that time, my guide, Augustus, was obviously very upset, but he did not know what to do. I told the gentleman that I was ready to go to the station, so off we went. The station was only a few blocks away; he ushered me into the office of the chief of police, a large, dark black man with a scowl on his face. He looked at me and said, "What are you doing in our country?" I told him that I was in the nation at the invitation of the president. He seemed very doubtful, but I just happened to have the president's letter inviting me to visit the nation in my pocket. I handed the letter to him; he looked it over, looked at me, looked at the gentleman who had arrested me, and replied that this was obviously a misunderstanding and that I was free to go.

Again, that is a lesson: it is not bad being the guest of the president in any country.

On another occasion, President Tolbert invited me to bring my wife, Beverly, along for my visit. I made airline reservations, flying from Houston to New York and then to Madrid, Spain. In Madrid, we were to transfer to an airliner going to Monrovia. On my previous trips I had never needed travel documents, other than my passport. On this occasion, however, after Beverly and I landed and made our way to our flight to Monrovia, we were stopped by a Spanish official who demanded to see our visas. I explained that we did not have visas and that I did not believe visas were necessary in that we were traveling as guests of and at the specific invitation of the President of Monrovia. I even provided the letter from the Monrovian president as proof. The government official, a small, stern woman, was not impressed. She looked me in the eye and said, "No visa, no plane."

While we were debating the issue, unfortunately, our plane and our luggage departed for Liberia, leaving us stranded in Madrid. Through help from the American Embassy, I was able to obtain a Liberian visa and was accommodated on the next plane to Monrovia, unfortunately with no luggage.

Upon arriving in Liberia, I attended a few meetings with government officials, while Beverly took a tour of Monrovia. Soon after my meetings, Augustus informed me that the president requested that Beverly and I be guests of honor at an investiture of two new members of his cabinet. Beverly was located and informed of the appointed time and place we were to attend. She was very reluctant since her only attire was a sundress and sandals due to the loss of our luggage. Though I tried to beg off, the president insisted he wanted us present. As we entered, Beverly and I noticed that it was obviously a very dressy event. All the ladies, mostly wives of ministers, were clad in their finery with long dresses, decorations for their hair, and plenty of jewelry. Beverly gave me a stare as we were entering, reminding me that she, unlike all the other ladies, was dressed only in her sundress and sandals.

Attempting to be inconspicuous, Beverly and I found seating towards the back of the chamber. Unfortunately, President Tolbert sent someone to summon us to the very front to join his party, requiring us to walk the length of the large hall and be seated to the president's right to Beverly's embarrassment. The postscript of this trip was that, after about four months, we finally received our luggage. Unfortunately, it looked like it had been underwater for several days and was ruined with mildew or worse.

Tragically, my representation contract with Liberia was terminated along with my client, President Tolbert. On my last trip to Liberia, President Tolbert informed me there was an ever-growing indication there would be some sort of revolution attempted or an attempted forceful turnover of the leadership of Liberia.

Liberia had been created through the United States' purchase of the territory from France on the west corner of Africa. The purpose of the purchase was to repatriate freed slaves and return them to Africa. The first nine presidents of Liberia were born in America, and its government thereby was patterned after the United States. The repatriated slaves of Africa were even in modern times referred to as "settler" families as opposed to native families. Because most of the repatriated slaves had useable skills and more education, they gained wealth more quickly than the native inhabitants as well as more of the government jobs that were created.

Consequently, there was long-standing unrest because of the great disparities of wealth in the country. I was able to arrange a meeting of President Carter's national security advisor, primarily through the help of Sarah Weddington, an old friend with whom I had served in the state legislature. After receiving the proper clearances, I was admitted to the White House and had a face-to-face meeting with Brezinsky. I informed him of President Tolbert's concern, particularly because Liberia had no army and a very weak police force, armed only with leftover M-1 rifles from WWII, most of which were inoperable. Brezinsky informed me he realized that Liberia was one of America's best friends in Africa and was even the location of the transmitter for the Voice of America in that world quadrant.

Unfortunately, I had to report to President Tolbert my lack of success. Brezinsky informed me that the various national security agencies and the CIA were keeping a close eye on matters in Liberia and that there would probably be no uprising. Less than two or three months after my visit to the White House, President Tolbert along with his cabinet were captured, hauled in a truck to the beach, lashed to poles, and machine gunned to death. I was shocked to see people whom I had known, visited, and dined with hanging limply from telephone poles and riddled with bullet holes.

The dirty deed had been done by Sergeant Doe. Sergeant Doe was a member of the contingent assigned to protect the president. Sergeant Doe and others for some time had been romanced by a gentleman claiming to be a Kubota tractor dealer. He would regularly host weekly poker nights, entertaining the sergeants with food, drink, and other benefits.

Unknown to the sergeant and others, the dealer was in fact an agent for Russia. For only $15,000, Sergeant Doe was persuaded to enter the president's compound and carry out the slaying of the leading government officials. I suspect that had I been in Liberia at the time, staying at the presidential guest house, which was my practice, I might have been one of Sergeant Doe's victims along with the others.

The Russian plan was to have Doe assassinate President Tolbert and then move into his place an agent who had been training for years in Moscow as the new president and leader of Liberia. Fortunately, the CIA did come to some semblance of rescue by convincing Sergeant Doe that, since he had led the revolt and assassinated the president himself, he should become the president. Appealing to Doe's ego was successful, and Sergeant Doe informed the Russians their choice to be the new leader had best vacate Liberia, or Doe would do to him what he had done to President Tolbert.

Following the president's assassination, Liberia suffered multiple civil wars with widespread slaughters of Liberian citizens and unrest for several years. Unfortunately for Doe, not many months into his leadership, he was captured and slain with a machete by another of the Liberian warlords. One of the disheartening things I learned later was that President Tolbert's son, A.B. Tolbert, with whom I had become good friends, had taken refuge in the French Embassy. Unfortunately, Doe and his crew ignored international law, invaded the Embassy, captured the younger Tolbert, dragged him into the street, and lopped off his head with a machete.

A lesson I learned from these tragedies was how fragile a democracy can be. Liberia was patterned exactly after our American style of government with a president, vice-president, congress, and supreme court but was done away with virtually overnight by a relatively small group of thugs. While democratic politics is rough, I think none of it compares to the way changing leadership was affected in this African nation.

Adventures in the Music Industry

Shortly after the judge threw out my indictment, which had been well publicized throughout Texas, I received a call from a gentleman named Sherwood Crier. Sherwood, I learned, was the owner and operator of Gilley's Club in Pasadena, Texas. Sherwood had quite a reputation as a showman and purveyor of musical talent. He also was somewhat famous for allegedly having invented a mechanical bull, which was featured in the movie *Urban Cowboy* along with his dance hall in Pasadena. Sherwood told me that he had been indicted for attempted murder and that, having followed my saga through the press, decided I had the grit to fight the local establishment and defend him. We agreed on a fee which was substantial and delivered to me in cash in a paper sack.

His indictment came about because of an incident at his dancehall. Apparently, in Pasadena, a tough guy, who was well known to be a karate expert and somewhat of a bully, became engaged in a dispute at Gilley's Club and ended up beating up one of Sherwood's customers, causing him serious injury. A few days later, the karate expert was attempting to leave his place of business not far from Gilley's, and someone began shooting at him with a shot gun. The karate expert escaped into his building, but apparently the shooter took out his frustration on the vehicle, shooting large holes throughout the gentleman's new Pontiac.

The tough guy filed a complaint, and police investigated. The police used tracking dogs. They sniffed a trail from Gilley's Club to the karate expert's studio. Based on this thin evidence and Sherwood's reputation, Sherwood was indicted.

While investigating charges against Sherwood, I became intimately familiar with the inside operation of Gilley's Club. His office was more like a museum of country music stars who had appeared. He had Willie Nelson's mug shot when he was arrested in Pasadena on a marijuana charge enlarged and framed and hanging on the wall over his desk. I was invited to sing a couple of songs with one of the star bands that was performing there. I did so and received an appropriate round of applause. As I left the stage, Sherwood was standing there, and I asked him what he thought of my performance. He dryly remarked, "Well, it wasn't too bad, nobody left."

My investigation and discovery filed with the appropriate court revealed very little evidence to support the charges against Sherwood. Eventually, the charges were dismissed. I think he was initially charged just because of Sherwood's reputation as being the leader of all bad things and even some crimes in Pasadena. My argument to the assistant district attorney was that I could prove that Sherwood was not guilty of attempted murder. When asked how, I argued to him that, if Sherwood had in mind to murder someone, that person would be dead. He laughingly agreed and dismissed the charges.

Only a few months later, I learned from Sherwood that he had been sued by Gilley. The original agreement between Gilley and Sherwood was that, if Gilley, who was a hot performer on the piano, would appear regularly at the club, Sherwood would name the club for him. Gilley sued based on some theory that, because Sherwood had named the club Gilley's, he should have a substantial interest in the club. I offered to represent Sherwood again, but he hired a top-notch business lawyer in Houston. The long and short of that story was that they were unsuccessful at trial and a huge judgment was entered against Sherwood.

At that point, Sherwood called me and begged me to take over the defense of the case, including an appeal. Again, my fee was delivered to me in cash in a paper lunch bag. I soon learned that the judge before whom the case had been tried was a racehorse afficionado and that the opposing lawyer, Tom Alexander, owned a ranch in Kentucky where he housed the judge's horses at no fee to.

During the appeal, Gilley filed another suit, and the judge appointed a receiver and ordered that all receipts at Gilley's Club be taken by the receiver, out of which he would pay his own very handsome fee and hold the rest in trust until the matter had been resolved.

***

The trustee was somewhat calloused in the way he operated. He would arrive at Gilley's Club unannounced, march to where the cash was kept, scoop it up, and depart with little, or no, accounting. I complained about his methods as well as the fact that he was leaving not enough to pay the overhead and was threatening the whole operation. When refused to relent with his methods, I filed suit against the trustee. The trustee later complimented me on the fact that I was the only lawyer who had threatened and had guts enough to really file suit against him. The short of a very long story, after many motions and multiple hearings before the court as well as the appellate court, we won the appeal. But during the very lengthy litigation, Gilley's Club burned to the ground. Of course, again, with Sherwood's reputation, a vast majority of folks in Harris County assumed that Sherwood was guilty of arson. Fortunately, for Sherwood, Pasadena police uncovered facts that a group of teenage boys had broken into Gilley's and ended up lighting a fire to cover up their burglary. We eventually settled all the disputes between Gilley and Sherwood by conveying to Gilley a small piece of property located in another state.

Another performer, Johnnie Lee, had a contract with Sherwood. Inspired by Gilley's lawsuit (in my opinion), he filed a suit against Sherwood. The suit was similar to the one filed by Gilley except it did not claim an interest in the club but claimed he had been short-changed on his agreement with Sherwood. Johnnie Lee was a hot prospect in that he had been featured in the movie and had produced a number one hit country and western song entitled, "Looking for Love in All the Wrong Places." Fortunately for Sherwood, and unfortunately for Johnnie Lee, we prevailed in that lawsuit, and not only did Johnnie Lee fail to recover any damages, he ended up on our cross claim having to pay Sherwood $100,000 and return to him a new Mercedes which had been part of the agreement for Sherwood's representation.

Another one of my adventures involving myself in music legends or stars was the fact that I was called on to handle Janis Joplin's estate as it existed in Texas. Janis' mother was far different from Janis. Mrs. Joplin was registrar at Port Arthur College and looked every bit like you would imagine a librarian or clerk for a college would look: little makeup, hair in a bun, very staid and conservative in her dress. I had also been acquainted with other musicians out of Austin, one of whom had been Janis' college roommate. The estate handling was somewhat routine except for the fact that Janis had acquired a $200,000 insurance policy from ASCAP with a double indemnity clause for accidental death. ASCAP is the association that enforces copyrights for musicians on music produced, recorded, or written. I sent in a claim on the insurance policy which was rejected by ASCAP on the grounds that Janis had willfully taken her own life. Fortunately for Janis, at least fortunately for her heirs, a younger brother and sister, the coroner in California had held an inquest and found Janis' death to be because of an accidental overdose of narcotics. The word accidental in the official coroner's report prevailed, and I was able to collect double indemnity payments and deliver them to the brother and sister, the rightful beneficiaries.

Probably the most unique and interesting adventure of my legal career involving musicians was the representation of one of my pals and, at the time, my barber, Chase Canfield. Chase was a good musician and a good barber. Chase approached me in my law office on Stadium Road and told me that he had a serious problem. Chase, in addition to being a musician, would book other musical appointments or concerts for which he earned a fee. For many years Chase contracted for musical entertainment at the Brad Club in Orange. The Brad Club was an organization for Dupont employees and had always had a huge Christmas time celebration. Chase made a good fee.

Chase reasoned that, since Fats Domino had contracted to appear at the Brad on Saturday night, he could earn some extra cash by promoting Fats at a concert at Lamar University in Beaumont. He did so, advertised the event, printed the tickets, and had great sales. The place was virtually sold out for a gymnasium at Lamar. Unfortunately for Chase, the concert was about to begin without Fats. Upon calling Fats, Chase was told that Fats had been busy changing the type of airplane preparing to make his trek to Beaumont. Although the plane was on its way, he had ordered dinner to go and would not leave until that time and would be somewhat late for the concert at Lamar. Even though Chase was on pins and needles waiting, by 10:30 and then 11:00 Domino had not appeared.

Eventually, Chase was called to the airport where a huge twin-engine plane landed and only 3 people got off, one of which was Fats. By the time Chase got him to the location of the concert, over half the people had left demanding their money back. And Fats had been drinking a lot. He did not give much of a concert, playing four or five tunes before he left the stage. Chase reimbursed a lot of money.

So, in my office, Chase inquired of me whether or not there was a way that I could recoup the money that he had to pay Domino to appear at the Friday night event. Chase informed me that the practice of such musicians was to demand payment in advance or they would not perform. And, that if he failed to pay Domino for Friday, he would not appear at the Saturday night event at which Chase had a huge fee awaiting him. I informed Chase that it would be very difficult to prosecute a lawsuit against Domino in that he was a resident of the state of Louisiana and would be gone with the money as soon as the concert was over and that he had a chartered airplane waiting for him to return home. Chase said that he would give it some thought and let me know if he figured any way out.

On Monday morning, Chase appeared chuckling to himself, telling me that he managed to keep the money from Domino. When the concert was to begin in Orange, Chase came up and offered Domino a check, Domino refused it, threatened to not go on stage, and reminded Chase that the deal was cash only. Chase said that he had trouble getting his money out of the bank, but that, if Domino would go ahead and play, he had a friend who owned a supermarket who was going to cash a check for him, and he could return by the first break of the evening with all the cash.

Reluctantly, Domino agreed to do so, but insisted his road manager would need to accompany Chase back to Port Arthur to cash the check. Thereafter, Chase and the road manager traveled to Port Arthur, pulled up to Sabine Bank, and began to share directly out of the bottle of bourbon that Chase had brought along. They were chit-chatting and sipping the bourbon when a Port Arthur policeman arrived, spotlighted the two of them in the vehicle, and inquired as to why they, in the middle of the night, were parked behind a bank. Chase told him it was very simple; they were waiting to cash a check. The policeman then asked for ID and noted that the road manager's ID showed his residence to be New York City. The policeman said that this was so suspicious that they would have to accompany him to the Port Arthur police station so that he could investigate the whole scenario further. Long story short, they were released just in time to see the end of the concert back in Orange.

When explaining to Fats what had happened, Domino glared at his road manager and said, "You fool, I would have arrested you myself." Of course, Domino filed suit, which was later changed to an arbitration case under the rules of ASCAP, which we defended and ultimately won. We argued that we were entitled to recoup the money that would have been paid for the Orange event because of the poor performance, or lack of performance Friday night at Lamar. Domino's lawyer argued through the arbitrator that it was just an old lawyer's trick to avoid payment of a just debt by arguing that we were owed for another event. After I told Chase that we had won the case, Chase attempted to prevail on me to send another letter to the lawyer defending Domino and tell him the old lawyer's trick had worked once again.

An Extraordinary Life for an Ordinary Man

This collection of bits and pieces of my mind started off as a note to my children and grandchildren. But then it started growing. At first, I couldn't stop. But then I wanted nothing more than to stop.

When I reflect on the arrangement of this book, I wish that one of those sections of my life would have been boring. In my memory of the times and my memory of how I felt at the times, I seemed to have kept busy. What all of the sections of my adult life have in common is surprise. Surprise keeps you busy. Of course, I tried to keep surprise at a minimum by being prepared. Preparation may score a run or two against surprise, but it can't win the game. Surprise seems to come back in the ninth. However, surprise brings some excitement with its stress. And caught in surprise, I kept busy trying to deal with surprise. And in business comes some amusement, even if from looking back at it.

So, though I am fully grateful for all the sections of my life, I believe that my law career had more surprises, and thus more amusement. Had I had just my law career, I would still be amused and content. It was enough. But my political career(s) and just my being alive when and where I was gave me an extraordinary life. What all these sections of my life had in common was that they "forced" opportunities to associate quite closely with a wide variety of people. As I explained, I simultaneously was involved with a judge, the supreme court, and man who crapped in a bucket. I saw what money did to and for people and what it made them into. I saw people from every rung of the social ladder.

Thus, at my age, I might have earned some boredom. So, these reminisces are ways to recreate and maybe approximate some safer surprise, excitement, stress, and busyness.

I wanted this book to end. But I just got tired. Writing is hard work. But I feel like I should add something, come to a point, or at least offer some insight or homily or advice. I'm not sure what it is, but I'll take some guesses.

In my memory, the people who do well or help other people or get something proper done, have ethics, beliefs, party affiliation, loyalties, and supporters but were able to overcome them. That statement above must sound like the sophistry that people assume is the property of "lawyers" and "politicians." But I'm not so much talking about sophistry—or betrayal—but constant examination of your position and of time and change. A careful lawyer or politician should be very careful of calcified beliefs, ethics, loyalties, supporters, etc. It's hard to do the good, the right, or the pragmatic thing. That's why, if it's simple, and you rely too much on what you don't question, then you probably won't do the good, the right, or the pragmatic thing. I think this attitude accounts for my wish to clean up all those calcified laws in our calcified constitution. Texas minds and legislation has become even more calcified since my time.

And, as I sifted through my memory to get this down, I saw that what got me through my careers and difficulties was an ability to shift course. You can't see what your career will throw at you, but you can stay nimble and be as ready as you can for change. You need both homework and observation to stay nimble.

Finally, as a lawyer and a politician, I had to know law and rules. But most of my success and most of my enjoyment came from people. I was constantly amused by them, even the bad ones. Unlike law and rules, you can't know them all, but you just ought to be ready for all their variety.

So maybe this collection of memories is for my children after all. It is a little bit of a road map to at least one person. And it is best read by those trying to navigate through their lives or careers. So, I hope that readers find some good ways and a few bad ways to set their courses and to face up to what might confront them.

Appendix 1: Photographs

Top: Carl Parker during a filibuster
Bottom: Parker with Governor Mark White

Queen Elizabeth II with Governor Anne Richards

Top: Governor Anne Richards with Lt. Governor Bob Bullock
Bottom: Parker swearing in for Governor for the Day

Top: Governor Dolph Briscoe
Bottom: Governor Clements

Governor Mark White

Top: UT Chancellor Hans Mark
Bottom: Governor Clements with Lt. Governor Hobby

Top: Killer Bees
Bottom: Bob Bullock

Top: Killer Bees returning
Bottom: Senator Judith Zaffrini

Rep. Craig Washington

Top: Senate education staff
Bottom: Lt. Governor Hobby

Top: Senator Gonzalo Barrientos
Bottom: Senate staff

Appendix 2: Staff Legislature

House Staff

Norma W. Bagelmam
Janice Barker
Mary Bates
Paul C. Guidry
Lettie Fay Bland
Bari J. Waldman
Lana Sharon Pinnell
Kathy L. English
William C. Brauder
Charlene S. Shrake
Alison L. Smith
Norita "Rita" Tillinghast
Sandra C. Marino
Patsy Jean Crannell
Mary Ellen Brown
Sara Lee Speights
Dora Gandy McDonald
Kyle Dennie Barrows
Mary Frances Roe
Eleanor Grace Lavelle
Rose Day

Senate Staff

Alicia Anderson
Mary E. Smith
Dr. Tom Sanders, (advisor, Lamar professor)
Patricia Gersbach
Mark Rosenthal
Maureen Roberts
Ed Restrepo
Caryn Cosper
David Gonzales
Melanie Leschber
Jennifer Mohn (Haley)
James Flelds
Tissie Stansbury
Cheryl Tripplett

Rhonda Talley
Donna Anderson
Suzanne J. Warmack
Marty Conway
Ursula Monroe
Linda Lassiter
Loretta Lewis
Geneva Johnson
Don Lamb
Geneva Johnson
Mark Bateman
Committee Staff
Calendars Committee
Arthur K. Vance
Financial Institutions
Dora McDonald
Education Committee
Sally Haenelt Cain
Dr. Terry Heller
Ronda Talley
Jerry Sanders
William B. Peacock
Suzanne Warmack
Ursula Monroe
Donna Anderson
Debbie Greene
Yvette Brun (Williams)
Stephanie Kurcheck

Economic Development Subcommittee on Insurance

C. J. Parham Tredway
Barbara Henderson
James Fields
Preston Hutson
Pamela Crail
Chelby King
Senior Interns
Luverda Batiste
Helen Huckaby
Majorie Young
James J. Wagner

Appendix 3: Parker Resume

Born August 6, 1934, in Port Arthur, Texas

Attended public school through high school

Graduate of University of Texas with degree in Economics (1956-entered law school after 3 years undergraduate)

Graduate of University of Texas Law School (1958)

Served in the U. S. Navy as a legal officer, stationed in Corpus Christi, TX

While in the navy, married Beverly Stiegler—married now 59 years.

They have 3 children, 4 grandchildren

Has practiced law for 62 years in Port Arthur, Texas

Elected to the Texas House of Representatives in 1962

Elected to the Texas Senate in 1976 where he served through 1994

He passed important legislation dealing with safety for children, education, issues related to workers and the public good

After retiring from the legislature, he continued to practice law until 2022

He writes regularly for the local *Penny Record* newspaper and stays involved in local politics in trying to "clean things up."

Loves music and loved to sing and perform until his vocal chords were damaged in the aftermath of surgery.

Has recently taken up woodcarving—birds, people, wildlife.

Is a voracious reader.

Appendix 4: Legislation Passed with Carl Parker as the Primary Author for the 58th through 73rd Legislatures

73rd Regular Session

SB 4
Caption: Relating to product liability.
SB 84
Caption: Relating to the payment date of certain public utility assessments and utility service and related service provided by or to the state, a state agency or institution, or a local government.
SB 175
Caption: Relating to the authority of the Commission on Jail Standards to regulate the temporary housing of county inmates in certain facilities to alleviate overcrowding in county jails.
SB 176
Caption: Relating to the adoption of the Durable Power of Attorney Act.
SB 179
Caption: Relating to hunting in state parks.
SB 201
Caption: Relating to contractual agreements between the Texas Higher Education Coordinating Board and Texas Chiropractic College and Parker College of Chiropractic
SB 336
Caption: Relating to prohibiting certain extensions of credit by retail stores owned or operated by public institutions of higher education.
SB 338
Caption: Relating to authorizing as a condition of parole or release to mandatory supervision for certain releases that the releases submit to treatment or counseling for substance abuse.
SB 339
Caption: Relating to the qualifications of sheriffs.
SB 394
Caption: Relating to the promotion of economic development in the state by improving the competitiveness of Texas public ports with ports outside of Texas, by extending the authority of navigation districts to sell or lease certain property of such districts.

SB 336
Caption: Relating to prohibiting certain extensions of credit by retail stores owned or operated by public institutions of higher education.

SB338
Caption: Relating to authorizing as a condition of parole or release to mandatory supervision for certain releases that the releases submit to treatment or counseling for substance abuse

SB339
Caption: Relating to the qualifications of sheriffs.

SB394
Caption: Relating to the promotion of economic development in the state by improving the competitiveness of Texas public ports with ports outside of Texas, by extending the authority of navigation districts to sell or lease certain property of such districts.

SB396
Caption: Relating to the organization and regulation of state savings banks; providing penalties.

SB 485
Caption: Relating to training for members of the governing boards of institutions of higher education.

SB 498
Caption: Relating to the continuation of the Public Utility Commission of Texas and the Office of Public Utility Counsel.

SB 654
Caption: Relating to college board advanced placement tests and courses and to establishing the Texas Advanced Placement Incentive Program.

SB 1041
Caption: Relating to protecting public drinking water supplies; creating offenses and providing fees and penalties.

SB 1042
Caption: Relating to the regulation of on-site sewage disposal systems; providing penalties.

SB 1043
Caption: Relating to the regulation of radioactive source material recovery,processing, and disposal activities and establishing and appropriating fees; transferring functions and appropriations.

SB 1049
Caption: Relating to the prevention of, the damage, cleanup, and costs related to, and liability for oil spills in coastal waters of the state; providing for response to the discharge of oil and other pol-

lutants in the coastal waters of the state; authorizing an appropriation from the coastal protection fund.

SB 1051

Caption: Relating to the reduction of solid waste by creating markets for recycled materials and otherwise promoting recycling and the use of recycled materials and by municipal solid waste management.

SB 1061

Caption: Relating to the continuation and functions of the Texas Board of Chiropractic Examiners and to the regulation of the practice of chiropractic; providing penalties.

SB 1062

Caption: Relating to the continuation and operation of the Texas State Board of Medical Examiners and to the regulation of the practice of medicine, including the practice of acupuncture; creating an offense and providing penalties.

SB 1072

Caption: Relating to the conveyance by the General Land Office of the state's interest in certain real property previously conveyed by the state to the city of Port Arthur.

SB 1073

Caption: Relating to the time of operation of water skis, aquaplanes and similar devices.

SB 1074

Caption: Relating to lights and sound-producing devices on a vessel or motorboat.

SB 1075

Caption: Relating to payment of fees for registration and licensing under Title 79, Revised Statutes.

SB 1326

Caption: Relating to the creation, administration, powers, and authority of the Chambers County Improvement District No. 1; granting the authority to issue bonds.

SB 1329

Caption: Relating to the administration of jails.

SB 1372

Caption: Relating to purchases and contracts of the Jefferson County Drainage District No. 7 and the authority of the manager of the district to hire and terminate employees of the district.

SB 1373

Caption: Relating to the creation, administration, powers, including taxing powers, duties, operations, financing, and dissolution

of the Town Center Improvement District of Montgomery County, Texas, and the power of certain entities to contract with the district.
SB 1409
Caption: Relating to medical liability actions and medical liability insurance; providing penalties.
SB 1410
Caption: Relating to state indemnification of and liability insurance premiums for certain health care claims.
SB 1424
Caption: Regulation of psychologists and to the continuation of the Texas State Board of Examiners of Psychologists; providing penalties.
SB 1425
Caption: Relating to the regulation of marriage and family therapists and to the continuation and operation of the Texas State Board of Examiners of Marriage and Family Therapists; providing penalties.
SB 1426
Caption: Relating to the regulation of social workers and to the creation of a new state board to replace the Council for Social Work Certification.

72nd Regular Session

SB 14
Caption: Relating to the prevention of, and the damage, cleanup, costs, and liability for, oil spills in coastal waters of the state; providing for adequate response to spills of oil and other pollutants in coastal waters; levying a coastal protection fee; creating the coastal protection fund; amending licensing requirements for pilots in state waters; making appropriations; and providing civil and criminal penalties.
SB 351
Caption: Relating to public schools.
SB 366
Caption: Relating to the payment of wages.
SB 408
Caption: Relating to certain officers of the court appearing and pleading in certain courts.
SB 409
Caption: Relating to further detention of certain persons.

SB 410
Caption: Relating to the administration of county jails.
SB 411
Caption: Relating to the definition of peace officers; making certain technical corrections.
SB 526
Caption: Relating to the conversion of certain hospital districts into districts operating under Article IX, Section 9, of the Texas Constitution.
SB 595
Caption: Relating to the change of domicile of insurance companies and health maintenance organizations.
SB 654
Caption: Relating to personal property exempt from seizure.
SB 815
Caption: Relating to compulsory pilotage services to or from ports in this state; imposing a civil penalty.
SB 843
Caption: Relating to the degree-granting authority of Lamar University at Port Arthur and Lamar University at Orange.
SB 932
Caption: Relating to the detachment and annexation of certain territory from a school district.
SB 933
Caption: Relating to the purchase of library books and materials for libraries at institutions of higher education.
SB 1287
Caption: Relating to the health professions resource center.
SB 1340
Caption: Relating to recycling programs and incentives; creating offenses and providing penalties.
SB 1341
Caption: Relating to the regulation of persons engaged in removing asbestos from public buildings or disturbing, encapsulating, or enclosing that asbestos; providing penalties.
SB 1342
Caption: Relating to the authority of a risk pool established by a political subdivision to obtain reinsurance.
SB 1343
Caption: Relating to the election of commissioners of the Port of Beaumont Navigation District of Jefferson County.
SB 1543
Caption: Relating to flood prevention and control; making appropriations.

SB 1554
Caption: Relating to establishing the Texas Academy of Leadership in the Humanities at Lamar University.
SB 1612
Caption: Relating to appointment, service, and duties of masters in proceedings for court-ordered mental health services.

72nd 1st Called Session

SB 2
Caption: Relating to the oversight and regulation of the state's environmental resources, natural resources, and energy resources; providing for the issuance of bonds by mitigation project participants; creating offenses and providing civil and criminal penalties.

71st Regular Session

SB 78
Caption: Relating to the expenditure of constitutionally appropriated funds at Lamar University at Port Arthur and Lamar University at Orange.
SB 95
Caption: Relating to school guidance counselors.
SB 96
Caption: Relating to foreign exchange teachers.
SB 134
Caption: Relating to security for judgments pending appeal.
SB 170
Caption: Relating to the operation of a vehicle with a child in the open bed of the vehicle and to the operation of a vehicle with a child not secured by a child passenger safety seat system; providing a penalty.
SB 199
Caption: Relating to addition of the environment as an initial priority research area supported by an advanced technology program.
SB 276
Caption: Relating to the operation of a moving vessel or the manipulation of water skis, an aquaplane, or other waterborne device while intoxicated; providing criminal penalties.
SB 457
Caption: Relating to funding higher education and the composition, continuation, and functions of the Texas Higher Education Coordinating Board.

SB 650
Caption: Relating to technology and telecommunications in public education.
SB 657
Caption: Relating to the personal civil liability of a member of the emergency management council or a local emergency planning committee.
SB 835
Caption: Relating to fees and deposits of institutions of higher education.
SB 937
Caption: Relating to Texas Water Development Board appointments to the board of directors of the Lower Neches Valley Authority.
SB 938
Caption: Relating to the jurisdiction of the 344th District Court.
SB 1019
Caption: Relating to the funding of elementary and secondary education.
SB 1047
Caption: Relating to the construction of statutes.
SB 1049
Caption: Relating to a central repository of school district boundary information and maps.
SB 1146
Caption: Relating to the sale of certain real property in Jefferson County by Lamar University.
SB 1742
Caption: Relating to the liability of pilots rendering pilot services to or from ports located in Jefferson County or Orange County.
SB 1794
Caption: Relating to the terms of directors of the Port of Port Arthur Navigation District.
SB 1800
Caption: Relating to the terms of commissioners of the Orange County Navigation and Port District.
71st 1st Called Session
SB 50
Caption: Relating to the contract authority of the Jefferson County Drainage District No. 7.

71st 6th Called Session

SB 1
Caption: Relating to public education.

70th Regular Session

SB 39
Caption: Relating to the creation, purpose, powers and duties, and funding of a hazardous waste research center at Lamar University at Beaumont.
SB 46
Caption: Relating to the name of the Port of Beaumont Navigation District of Jefferson County.
SB 318
Caption: Relating to the definition of net assets as it applies to certain insurers.
SB 335
Caption: Relating to testing public school teachers and administrators.
SB 367
Caption: Relating to the exemption of recreational boats from ad valorem taxation.
SB 437
Caption: Relating to the authority of the Texas Housing Agency to issue bonds and to enter into certain agreements.
SB 537
Caption: Relating to the health risk assessment of certain toxic substances and harmful physical agents by the Texas Department of Health.
SB 543
Caption: Relating to reporting of postsecondary academic performance to high schools.
SB 651
Caption: Relating to the relationship between a sales representative and the representative's principal.
SB791
Caption: Relating to student center fees at Lamar University.
SB 792
Caption: Relating to the exchange of certain property by Lamar University.

SB 994
Caption: Relating to teacher education.
SB 1024
Caption: Relating to the compensation of judges in Chambers County.
SB 1309
Caption: Relating to the employment of off-duty officers to monitor the taking of shellfish from polluted areas.
SB 1473
Caption: Suspending Senate rules to permit the Conference Committee on H.B. 685 to consider certain matters.
SR 709
Caption: Suspending Senate rules to permit the Conference Committee on H.B. 2181 to consider certain matters.

70th 2nd Called Session

SB 11
Caption: Relating to the name of the Beaumont Navigation District.
SB 86
Caption: Relating to the election of appointment of members of the State Board of Education.

69th Regular Session

SB 172
Caption: Relating to the membership of the Southern Regional Education Compact.
SB 257
Caption: Relating to the terms of court of the 344th District Court.
SB 483
Caption: Relating to certain reports made by pharmaceutical peer review or pharmaceutical organization committees that result in possible disciplinary or remedial action by the Texas State Board of Pharmacy and to certain powers of the board; relating to immunity from liability and presumption of good faith.
SB 578
Caption: Relating to higher education finance, including the appropriation and allocation of funds under Article VII, Section 17, of the Texas Constitution and the effective date of previously authorized tuition increases.

SB 611
Caption: Relating to ownership of library materials and equipment purchased with funds appropriated under the Library Systems Act; amending Section 15 Article 5446a, Vernon's Texas Civil Statutes.
SB 612
Caption: Relating to limitations on the authority of the State Purchasing and General Services Commission to acquire certain materials and services for libraries operated by university systems or institutions of higher education; amending Section 3.01, State Purchasing and General Services Act, as amended (Article 601b, Vernon's Texas Civil Statutes).
SB 716
Caption: Relating to the creation of political subdivisions in municipal industrial districts.
SB 854
Caption: Relating to adoption of a non-substantive revision of miscellaneous statutes relating to criminal procedure, including certain provisions for penalties; making conforming amendments and repeals.
SB 969
Caption: Relating to provision of housing for the elderly and to the powers and duties of the Texas Housing Agency, corporations organized under the Texas Housing Financing Corporation Act, and the Texas Department of Aging; creating a special fund and prescribing its use.
SB 1235
Caption: Relating to the composition of the State Textbook Committee.
SB 1282
Caption: Relating to the issuance of bonds by certain cities to pay current expenses; providing for the levy of a tax to pay the principal of an interest thereon; containing other provisions pertaining to the subject; and declaring an emergency.
SB 1330
Caption: Relating to the acquisition, development, and operation of certain islands and related facilities and improvements; providing for financing.
SB 1356
Caption: Relating to the creation, administration, powers, duties, operation, and financing of the Montgomery County Municipal Utility District No. 69; and declaring an emergency.
SB 1357
Caption: Relating to creation, administration, powers, duties, oper-

ation, and financing of the Montgomery County Municipal Utility District No. 70; and declaring an emergency.
SB 1358
Caption: Relating to the creation, administration, powers, duties, operation, and financing of the Montgomery County Municipal Utility District No. 71; and declaring an emergency.
SB 1359
Caption: Relating to the creation, administration, powers, duties, operation, and financing of the Montgomery County Municipal Utility District No. 72; and declaring an emergency.
SB 1360
Caption: Relating to the creation, administration, powers, duties, operation, and financing of the Montgomery County Municipal Utility District No. 73; and declaring an emergency.
SB 1361
Caption: Relating to the creation, administration, powers, duties, operation, and financing of the Montgomery County Municipal Utility District No. 74; and declaring an emergency.
SB 1458
Caption: Relating to creation, organization, boundaries, purposes, powers, duties, functions, authority, and financing of the Bastrop County Reclamation, Road, and Utility District, No. 1.
SR 160
Caption: Supporting cooperative programs between the Texas Housing Agency and the Texas Department on Aging.
SR 170
Caption: Directing the State Board of Education to revise the proposed definition of a grade reporting period.
SR 328
Caption: Directing the Senate Jurisprudence Committee to conduct an interim study of the State's system of legal representation.
SR 351
Caption: Expressing pride and gratitude to all older Texans and declaring May 1, 1985, as Senior Day.
SR 392
Caption: Requesting Lieutenant Governor appoint blue-ribbon committee to conduct interim study of State's system of securities regulation.
SR 481
Caption: Requesting State Board of Education to conduct study of existing school facilities in the State.

SR 483
Caption: Establishing delegation appointed by Lieutenant Governor to protest in Washington the proposed withholding and diversion of funds authorized for and allocated to States for water sports purposes.

68th Regular Session

SB 173
Caption: Relating to an aggravated or deadly assault on a jailer or a guard.
SB 215
Caption: Relating to creation, membership, powers, and duties of the Texas Diabetes Council and to the development of public awareness and training and to other duties by the Texas Department of Health, the Texas Commission for the Blind, the Texas Rehabilitation Commission, the Texas Department of Human Resources, and the Central Education Agency; providing that funds for travel reimbursement shall be appropriated to the department.
SB 409
Caption: Relating to the provision of physical facilities for Lamar University at Port Arthur and Lamar University at Orange.
SB 410
Caption: Relating to student centers and fees for student centers at Lamar University at Orange and Lamar University at Port Arthur.
SB 620
Caption: Relating to the Lamar University System and to certain appropriations by the legislature to Lamar University.
SB 621
Caption: Relating to the continuance of public hearings.
SB 763
Caption: Relating to contracting to provide for the transportation of public school students.
SB 799
Caption: Relating to student services fees at certain institutions of higher education.
SB 1125
Caption: Relating to absences from public school for religious holy days.
SB 1227
Caption: Relating to the exclusion of serial and journal subscriptions for certain libraries from the requirements of the State Purchasing and General Services Act.

SB 1283
Caption: Relating to the conversion of a navigation district acting under the provisions of Article III, Section 52 of the Constitution of the State of Texas into a navigation district acting under Article XVI, Section 59 of the Constitution of the State of Texas, to certain notice and hearing requirements, to elections, and to certain powers and duties of the commissioners' courts and of converted districts.

SB 1285
Caption: Relating to creation, judges, jurisdiction, powers and duties, personnel, facilities, and practice and procedure of the County Court at Law of Liberty County.

SB 1286
Caption: Relating to the creation, judges, jurisdiction, personnel, and powers and duties of the County Court of Jefferson County at Law No. 3 and to the jurisdiction, judges, personnel, and powers of the County Courts of Jefferson County Nos. 1 & 2.

SB 1314
Caption: Relating to the authority of the Jefferson County Drainage District No. 6 and participating entities to acquire property.

SB 1352
Caption: Relating to the appointment, duties, and staff of court administrators and their compensation, facilities, and equipment and the appointment, powers, and duties of masters for certain courts in Jefferson County.

SB 1356
Caption: Relating to the dissolution of the Northwest Harris County Municipal Utility District No. 7 and to certain powers and duties of the board of directors of the district.

SB 1375
Caption: Relating to establishment, membership, personnel, compensation, powers and duties, and financing of a juvenile board in Chambers County and to the appointment of an advisory council.

SB 1381
Caption: Relating to the creation, directors, administration, powers, duties, and financing of the Broussard Sewage District; requiring a confirmation election and allowing periodic elections; providing for extinguishment of the district unless confirmed within five years.

SB 1382
Caption: Relating to the creation, directors, administration, powers, duties, and financing of the Fannett Sewage District; requiring a confirmation election and allowing periodic elections; providing for extinguishment of the district unless confirmed within five years.

SB 1384
Caption: Relating to creation, directors, administration, powers, duties, and financing of the North Cheek Sewage District; requiring a confirmation election and allowing periodic elections; providing for the extinguishment of the district unless confirmed within five years.

SB 1385
Caption: Relating to the creation, administration, powers, duties, and financing of the South Cheek Sewage District; requiring a confirmation election and allowing periodic elections; providing for extinguishment of the district unless confirmed within five years.

SB 1386
Caption: Relating to the creation, directors, administration, powers, duties, and financing of the North LaBelle Sewage District; requiring a confirmation election and allowing periodic elections; providing for extinguishment of the district unless confirmed within five years.

SB 1387
Caption: Relating to the creation, directors, administration, powers, duties, and financing of the South LaBelle Sewage District; requiring a confirmation election and allowing periodic elections; providing for the extinguishment of the district unless confirmed within five years.

SR 249
Caption: Creating committee to meet with Washington staff of US Army Corps of Engineers to persuade Corps to rescind decision to close 59 lakeside parks in Texas

SR 532
Caption: Directing Texas Coastal and Marine Council to take action to assure maximum benefits to the State in securing oil and gas structures for artificial reefs to enhance fishery resources.

SR 672
Caption: Directing the Senate Finance Committee to monitor the changing need for recreational services in Texas.

8th 2nd Called Session
SB 3
Caption: Relating to child passenger safety seat systems, providing a penalty.

SR 46
Caption: Providing for the consideration of all bills concerning public education by the Committee of the Whole Senate on Education.

SB 18
Caption: Relating to hunting in Sea Rim State Park.

SB 211
Caption: Relating to tampering with equipment of or the unauthorized procuring, diversion, or use of services of public communication, public transportation, public water, gas, power supply, telecommunications, or other public service and the unauthorized use or manufacture, sale, or distribution to aid in the unauthorized use of subscription television decoding and interception devices; providing criminal and civil penalties and enforcement procedures.

SB 320
Caption: Relating to pilot programs and services for deaf-blind multi-handicapped individuals.

SB 418
Caption: Relating to the taking, possession, and sale of alligator's parts of an alligator; providing penalties.

SB 528
Caption: Relating to time off from work to attend political conventions.

SB 548
Caption: Amending Section 1, Chapter 379, Acts of the 63rd legislature, Regular Session, 1973, as amended, relating to the Sabine Pass Port Authority; confirming the creation of said authority, enlarging its boundaries, and authorizing bond assumption and maintenance tax elections in connection therewith, providing for the severability of the Act.

SB 565
Caption: Relating to regulation of private investigators and private security agencies and the disposition and use of funds; providing civil penalties.

SB 596
Caption: Relating to the creation or reorganization of certain judicial districts, to the terms of certain courts, and to the powers, duties, and compensation of judges and officers of certain county and district courts; relating to the creation and duties of prosecuting attorneys for certain districts and to their abolition in certain areas; relating to the composition of certain juvenile boards and to the jurisdiction of and other provisions for certain county and district courts; and making an appropriation.

SB 619
Caption: Relating to the waiver of certain provisions of the Deceptive Trade Practices-Consumer Protection Act, as amended, by certain consenting business concerns or consumers.
SB 658
Caption: Relating to prescriptions of controlled substances.
SB 710
Caption: Relating to public school contracts that require competitive bidding.
SB 747
Caption: Relating to the use of county equipment and employees to assist other governmental entities.
SB 749
Caption: Relating to the issuance of commercial bay shrimp boat licenses and commercial bait-shrimp boat licenses and to certain studies and reports.
SB 1016
Caption: Relating to authority to establish a foreign trade zone in the Port Arthur Customs District.
SB 1286
Caption: Authorizing the sale and conveyance or trade of certain land in Jefferson County by the Texas Department of Mental Health and Mental Retardation; providing for the use of proceeds; and declaring an emergency.

66th Regular Session

SB 39
Caption: Relating to medical, physical, or mental conditions preventing issuance or causing cancellation of a driver's license and preventing operation of a motor vehicle.
SB 130
Caption: Relating to the powers, duties, contracts and financing of the Port of Port Arthur Navigation District of Jefferson County, Texas.
SB 131
Caption: Relating to certain rights, privileges, duties, and powers of spouses.
SB 296
Caption: Relating to the establishment of a housing program for

families and individuals of low income and families of moderate income.

SB 489
Caption: Relating to lewd, immoral, or indecent conduct of persons on the premises of a retail beer establishment.

SB 846
Caption: Relating to offenses involving assault on a peace officer or a participant in a court proceeding.

SB 849
Caption: Relating to the manner of serving a subpoena.

SB 854
Caption: Relating to admonitions by the court to the defendant before accepting a plea of guilty or nolo contendere.

SB 855
Caption: Relating to requested special charges in criminal cases and the requirement that instructions be in writing.

SB 856
Caption: Relating to notice to the petitioner of a motion, answer, or other pleading filed by the attorney for the state in a habeas corpus proceeding or of orders of the court relating to the proceeding.

SB 890
Caption: Relating to the authority of general-law city or town to close a street or alley.

SB 891
Caption: Relating to the membership in the appointive office or employee class of the Employees Retirement System of Texas.

SB 893
Caption: Relating to the terms of court of the 253rd District Court.

SR 668
Caption: Establishing a special interim committee to study the current financial market and its effect on the housing situation in Texas.

SR 744
Caption: Extending congratulations to the veterans of the Vietnam War.

65th Regular Session

SB 285
Caption: To provide for at least four regular meetings per year in the state capital (instead of six) of the Texas Board of Mental Health and Mental Retardation; and declaring an emergency.

SB 336
Caption: Appropriating supplemental sums of money for the fiscal

year ending August 31, 1977, to pay the additional cost of purchased utilities (non-transferable) at certain public institutions of higher education; and declaring an emergency.

SB 446
Caption: Relating to examination requirements for certain applicants for a chiropractor's license.

SB 496
Caption: Relating to the use of school buses for non-school activities.

SB 637
Caption: Relating to changing the name of Lamar University at Jefferson and Orange Counties to Lamar University at Port Arthur and Lamar University at Orange.

SB 843
Caption: Relating to state financial assistance to local public agencies or nonprofit corporations that operate programs to recruit retired persons to perform volunteer community services.

SR 673
Caption: Directing the standing Committee on Intergovernmental Relations to study methods to make housing available to the poor.

65th 2nd Called Session

Extending congratulations to Mrs. Helen Dishongh.

64th Regular Session

HB 272
Caption: Relating to creating a Commission on Jail Standards and prescribing its powers, duties, and functions relating to the condition of county jails.

HB 431
Caption: Relating to the Private Investigators and Private Security Agencies Act; making the Act applicable to certain persons; relating to the duties and powers of the Texas Board of Private Investigators and Private Security Agencies; relating to the suspension or revocation of licenses or registration; prohibiting certain activities; relating to the qualification for licensure or registration; authorizing the commissioning of security officers; relating to training programs; relating to security bonds and liability insurance.

HB 1746
Caption: Relating to excusing persons who are members of the Jewish faith from school attendance on certain Jewish holidays;

providing that the persons shall be counted as attending average daily attendance.

63rd Regular Session

HR 58
Caption: Providing for hanging the reverse side of the Great Seal of the State of Texas in memory of the Honorable Will L. Smith.
HR 220
Caption: Creating an interim study committee concerning closed circuit television in relation to medical education.

62nd Regular Session

HB 130
Caption: Relating to the establishment and operation of an educational center of Lamar University in certain counties.
HB 132
Caption: Relating to the salaries of certain precinct officials in certain counties.
HB 136
Caption: Relating to the jurisdiction of the county courts at law of Jefferson County in certain civil matters and cases.
HB 453
Caption: Relating to safety of persons engaged in activities in the proximity of high voltage electric lines.
HB 572
Caption: Relating to the salary of the judge of the County Court of Jefferson County at Law No. 2.
HB 573
Caption: Relating to the salary of the Judge of the County Court of Jefferson County at Law.
HB 765
Caption: Relating to firemen or policemen receiving upon termination of their service, a lump-sum payment of the full amount of salary for accumulated sick leave and vacation leave.
HB 1777
Caption: Relating to authorizing notaries public who are stockholders of corporations owning less than 1/10 of one percent of the stock of a corporation of which there are more than 1,000 shareholders, or employees of such a corporation, to take acknowledgments of instruments in which such corporation is interested.

HCR 134
Caption: Granting National Marine Service permission to sue the state.
HR 266
Caption: Requesting certain state agencies and individuals to make an investigation and compile a report.
HR 442
Caption: Creating a committee to study the proper utilization and standard applications of automated data processing in state government.
HR 630
Caption: Creating a special interim committee on Insurance Benefits for City Employees.

62nd 2nd Called Session

HR 1
Caption: Providing procedure for election of Speaker of the House of Representatives.
HR 71
Caption: Naming Kelly Dan Kubiak a Mascot of the House of Representatives of the 62nd legislature.

62nd 3rd Called Session

HR 29
Caption: Authorizing the acceptance of a gift in memory of Representative Will L. Smith.

61st Regular Session

HB 185
Caption: Relating to the amounts to be paid and eligibility to receive certain benefits under the Firemen's Relief and Retirement Fund for fully paid fire departments in cities and towns having a population of less than 165,000.
HB 187
Caption: Relating to the payment of firemen and policemen who are required to appear in court as witnesses on their time off.

61st 1st Called Session

None

61st 2nd Called Session

None

60th Regular Session

HB 559
Caption: Relating to the occupational safety of employees of industry and enterprise; providing for enforcement and prescribing penalties; providing for cooperation with other state agencies.
HB 885
Caption: Relating to additional compensation for certain constables.

60th 1st Called Session

None

59th Regular Session

HB 418
Caption: Relating to amending certain statutes relative to fees in delinquent tax suits.
HB 652
Caption: Relating to providing that the Commissioners Court of Jefferson County, Texas, pay the Judges of the 58th Judicial District, the 60th Judicial District, the 136th Judicial District and Criminal District Court, compensation in addition to compensation paid by the State and providing the manner of payment thereof; providing for compensation to be paid by the Commissioners Court of Jefferson County to the Judge of the Court of Domestic Relations for Jefferson County, and providing the manner of payment thereof.

58th Regular Session

None

End Note

One of my favorite quotes comes from Samuel Clements: "When you see a turtle on a post, you know he had help getting there."

The interesting and rewarding life I have had has been made possible by the help from friends, family, and especially loyal employees. Coming from a home without running water, I feel blessed to have been able to put significant legislation on the books in Texas, engage in international associations with foreign nations and experience interesting events in my life.

I am gratified to my employees noted in this appendix and apologize to any whose name escapes me.

I hope that you and the family members I leave behind have enjoyed reading this book as much as I enjoyed writing it.

Printed in the USA
CPSIA information can be obtained
at www.ICGtesting.com
LVHW022027020824
787207LV00003B/686